THE BEATLES

1962-1969

FROM LIVERPOOL TO ABBEY ROAD

WHITE STAR PUBLISHERS

CONTENTS

INTRODUCTION

Who knows what the world would have been like without the Beatles? Would our lives be the same today? Would the cultural shifts and social revolutions taking place in the world between the 1960s and 1970s have been possible without the 'Fab Four'? Probably not. What is certain is that the world would have been sadder and less colorful, with far less hope and joy—two fundamental elements of the Beatles' philosophy. Is anyone capable of imagining the history of the twentieth century without the Beatles? No, though it must also be said that history books still do not give due consideration to the influence the Fabulous Four had on the development of Western society from the 1960s on. Here, we've created a brief over-

WHO KNOWS WHAT THE WORLD, AND OUR LIVES, WOULD HAVE BEEN LIKE WITHOUT THE BEATLES

view of everything the arrival of the Beatles generated on the world scene. Certain elements may seem minor in the long course of history, but the band's impact on the behaviors, lifestyles, and artistic forms of expression from the 1960s to the present have been spectacularly profound.

5 *A sequence of photo proofs of the band taken outdoors at the beginning of their careers.*

7 *George Harrison, John Lennon, Paul McCartney, and Ringo Starr behind the door of their dressing room before their concert at the Odeon Theatre in Manchester on May 30th, 1963.*

LET'S BEGIN WITH WHAT MAY SEEM LIKE AN ABSOLUTELY INSIGNIFICANT POINT—THE LENGTH OF THEIR HAIR

Let's begin with what may seem like an absolutely insignificant point—the length of their hair. The best-known Beatles hairstyle, still considered an identifying symbol of the band, is the 'mop-top'. Before the Beatles had reached the limelight, boys and men had their hair cut only one way: short, with the creative possibility of parting it to the left or the right. As a third option, they could slick their hair back à la Humphrey Bogart. That was about the extent of the choices. The Beatles' hair, on the other hand, was much longer than the unwritten rule, had no parting, and wasn't combed back at all. It was long and bowl-shaped, with bangs trimmed evenly on all sides. This hairstyle appeared in the early 1960s, and despite the fact that the band members were always well-groomed and neat, they were still considered 'longhairs' and 'rebels' compared to their parents and society in general. Actually, their hair wasn't that long, and if we stop to think about the number of persons with long, disheveled hair in literature and art before the Beatles, we certainly can't say that long hair was an original idea. But there are key differences: the Beatles in the early 1960s weren't dropouts, radicals, or revolutionaries—they were 'good lads', polite, cheerful, and likable. This image helped them reach, and ultimately become an example for, a huge worldwide public.

They related to an entire generation rather than to just a small group of poets and revolutionaries. They told teenagers, all teenagers, that they should let their hair grow long if they wanted to. And teenagers throughout the globe quickly got the message. A few years later, Jerry Rubin, one of the leaders of the creative and revolutionary hippy counterculture movement in the United States, once said: "Long hair is our black skin" in an attempt to explain that there was no simpler, more direct way to reveal your outlook and social stance. All you needed was long hair to automatically identfiy as an 'outsider'. And this happened primarily because the Beatles had broken a hairstyle rule. For years, they wore long hair as a sort of uniform, in part to declare that they belonged to another culture, as it were. These transitions occurred rapidly. The relatively neat mop-top, so fashionable in 1966, started to seem like a relic compared to the tousled hair common in 1968. From this point forward, Western society began to communicate through hairstyles, a trend that prevailed until the end of the 1980s, after which hair as a tool of communication in counterculture began to lose its edge. Nowadays, people dye their hair any color they please and maintain the most outrageous hairstyles without communicating or challenging anything at all. But if it weren't for the Beatles, we might still be wearing our hair in short, traditional styles and struggling with that critcal choice: do I part it to the left or to the right?

Without a doubt, the role the Beatles played in the spread of certain forms of spirituality and Eastern cultures is well-documented. It's fair to say that, within the framework and huge numbers of pop culture, the Beatles may have served as an introduction to India for an entire generation. Of course, the Beatles weren't the first Westerners to explore India's culture and music, but for the young people in Great Britain, America, and Europe, India still felt like a distant, little-understood place rarely visted by outsiders. The Beatles began experimenting with meditation through a ten-day conference held by the Spiritual Regeneration Movement in Bangor, Wales. This inspired them to travel to Rishikesh, in northern India, where they stayed for a few weeks meditating and writing music. The Western youth of the 1960s were not big travelers; they generally remained in their hometowns and, at most, went to the nearest big cities for doses of outside culture. This was a generation that learned about the world chiefly through books, radio, television, and records. The Beatles went to India, and when they returned, they challenged the youth of the West to seek out new experiences abroad. This worldview encouraged travel outside of hometowns and native countries, which, they believed, only had so much to offer in terms of spiritual direction and wisdom. They considered exchanges of foreign customs and beliefs to be a necessary part of understanding human nature. In short, it was time for the West to wake up to the fact that much of the world lived and prospered while maintaining very different lifestyles and philosophies.

George Harrison was fundamental to this change. His own spiritual evolution played a pivotal role in encouraging many young people to discover the Far East and Africa. If they weren't able to travel in person, he encouraged them to pay closer attention to the culture and art originating from these places, which was rapidly becoming more available in the West. India, above all, became a popular destination for people wishing to follow in the Beatles' spiritual footsteps. Its customs and religions took on a special allure due to the media frenzy surrounding visits by many American and British celebrities and the discovery of meditation on the part of Paul, John, and George (McCartney still currently practices transcendental meditation). These developments influenced the way much of the Western world viewed spirituality, meditation, and travel.

And drugs? Well, this is more complicated, as the damages wrought by the spread of drugs in our society is plain to see.

The Beatles did little to curb the spread of drugs throughout the 1960s. The simple fact is that they were very open with the media about their drug use, setting an example for many young people throughout the world and undoubtedly inspiring them to try the same drugs. There are many arguments for why this was damaging to society. It should be noted that their drug use inlcuded many different types of drugs, from amphetamine in the early 1960s to marijuana, LSD, cocaine, and heroin in later years (particularly regarding John Lennon). The only drug the Beatles actually promoted was LSD, or lisergic acid dithylamide, which, in their opinion, had a positive effect on their creative processes.

By the mid-1960s, LSD had become a favorite drug of the counterculture, which sought to broaden the "confines of consciousness" by any means necessary. The spread of LSD, especially in the United States, reached epidemic proportions among the young, who considered the pills an easier, more direct way to bring about spiritual experiences. Its use was encouraged by personalities such as Ken Kesey and Timothy Leary and depicted by the Beatles on the

THEIR MUSIC IS NOT OLD; IT IS not a 'museum piece', even though IT IS HISTORY WITH A CAPITAL 'H'

explosively colorful covers of the albums *Sgt. Pepper's Lonely Hearts Club Band* and *Magical Mystery Tour*. In this view, the drug's benefits weren't just personal. It could help revolutionize society as a whole by altering one's individual perception of the world. This altered perception was supposed to open up many new artistic opportunities and possibilities for mankind. The Beatles used LSD as a creative tool in order to discover parts of themselves that might have otherwise remained hidden. They never promoted the drug culture as such, and drugs were never at the center of their creative universe. But it's clear the band contributed to a worldwide phenomenon that caused lasting damage to an entire generation. Did they influence history? Most certainly.

Music is an easy one. When we think of rock, blues, the French *chanson*, or any of the other forms of music popularized from 1963 on, we can't help thinking of the innovations introduced by John Lennon, Paul McCartney, Ringo Starr, and George Harrison, nicknamed the 'Fabulous Four', the 'Fab Four', the 'Baronets', and the 'lads from Liverpool'. They invented the 'beat' and, together with Bob Dylan, are considered the fathers of rock music as we know it today. They wrote some of the loveliest and best-known songs of the 20th century and helped define their generation through their fashion and lifestyle choices. An entire generation grew its hair long thanks to the Beatles. They extended the confines of perception through meditation and more chemical means, and they pushed the boundaries of pop thanks to their willingness to incorporate instruments and recording techniques from many different styles of music. All of this was accomplished in less than ten years (between 1962 and 1970) on twelve historic albums.

To this day, the story of the Beatles inspires us. It's the story of four friends from the outskirts of Liverpool who conquered the world with guitars and drums and set an entire generation on fire. Only a few years after their formation, they became the most successful and popular band on Earth, sparking what became known as Beatlemania. Their first single, "Love Me Do," was released almost 60 years ago. John Lennon was killed in Manhattan in 1980, and George Harrison died in 2001 after a long illness. Ringo Starr and Paul McCartney continue to record and perform music. Paul in particular still makes sure to play plenty of Beatles tunes at his concerts. The band still smiles at us from countless posters and album covers. The pedestrian crossing on Abbey Road in England has become a national monument, visited every year by thousands of people from around the world. And of course their songs are still broadcasted continuously on TV, the radio, and through the Internet. Why? The reason is simple: the Beatles have such a grip on our collective imagination that the passage of time has done little to effect their image and popularity. Their songs have a unique quality that has allowed them to transcend time and the shifting of musical tastes. In short, while the world has become different, the power of their music has remained the same, and although their concerts and performances have become History with a capital H, their music continues to find fans in each new generation.

This book attempts to narrate the history of the Beatles, from the start of their careers to their conquering of America and the rest of the world. We'll also focus on the saga of their recordings and albums, their less-publicized achievements, and the final years of their collaboration. Undoubtedly, the band provided the soundtrack for a decades-long revolution—a revolution complete with long hair, miniskirts, flower power, and many other forms of psychedelia. This particular revolution began in the late 1950s in Great Britain, in a port city called Liverpool.

12-13 Pattie Boyd, Tina Williams, Prue Bury, and Susan Whitman combing the hair of George Harrison, Ringo Starr, Paul McCartney, and John Lennon during a break in the filming of A Hard Day's Night.

1

1956–1959
THE BEATLES
BEFORE THE BEATLES

FOUR YOUNGSTERS FROM LIVERPOOL PURSUING A BIG DREAM

Can we call them the Beatles before they were The Beatles? Perhaps, if we want to believe that the destiny of John, Paul, George, and Ringo was inevitable and that they were meant to meet each other and realize a project of tremendous influence on the world. What was this project all about? Beauty, imagination, change, hope, higher perception, and the transformation of rock music. Unbeknownst to them, their paths were meant to cross; the four were meant to meet each other and bring exuberance and joy to a post-WWII generation desparately in need of a spiritual lift.

John is often identified as the driving force, the nucleus, the one who brought most of the band together while they were still in high school. John Winston Lennon was born in Liverpool on October 9th, 1940. He was the 'founding father' of the band and sparked the inevitable chain of events which led to their early performances in Liverpool and Hamburg. His passion for music developed early, while he was still a student at Quarry Bank High School in Liverpool. In his early childhood, he played a harmonica a friend had loaned him. But the epiphany arrived when he listened to Rock 'n' Roll for the first time. He realized it was the world he belonged in, instead of the house on 251 Menlove Avenue in Liverpool that he had lived in with his Aunt Mimi since 1946. He was sixteen when he first heard Bill Haley, Elvis Presley, and, perhaps most importantly, skiffle played by Lonnie Donegan, sometimes called the poor English man's version of Rock 'n' Roll. Suddenly the rest of the world didn't make much sense to John.

JOHN WAS THE 'MOTOR' OF THE BAND, THE INDISPENSABLE ELEMENT IN THEIR FORMATION

But he needed an instrument in order to access this new world. Wth the help of his mother Julia, who loved music and played the banjo, he bought his first guitar for ten pounds, ordering it by mail after seeing an ad for it in a newspaper. He immediately set about forming a band with his schoolmates. They were called the Quarrymen, and by 1956, they were already playing small shows in Liverpool, mostly for their high school friends.

James Paul McCartney was born on June 18th, 1942, in Liverpool, to a family with a strong background in music. Paul's father James played in his own group, the Jim Mac's Jazz Band, and had a large collection of 78-rpm records. Although the McCartney family was not well off, they managed to buy a piano at Harry Epstein's North End Music Store in Liverpool. Paul's father encouraged him and his brother Mike to pursue their interests in music, and Paul learned to play the piano by ear and began writing his first songs. After the death of Paul's mother Mary, James McCartney gave Paul a trumpet, but jazz and other, more traditional forms of music were not his main passion. He had already fallen in love with Rock 'n' Roll—with Buddy Holly and the Crickets, Little Richard, and Bill Haley & His Comets. With his father's permission, Paul, at fourteen years old, sold his trumpet and purchased a guitar. He immediatley began learning how to play and sing at the same time so that he could start performing his own original songs.

George Harold Harrison was born on February 25th, 1943, in Liverpool, where he lived in a modest and crowded house. He was the baby of his large family. School didn't interest him much; it was music that stirred his passions and, encouraged by his mother, who recognized his precocious talent, he began taking music classes at an early age. His obsession with music led to a friendship with Paul McCartney, who was a year older and one of his schoolmates. They rode to school together on the same bus. George was similarly bewitched by this new wave of Rock 'n' Roll. One morning, as thirteen-year-old George was riding his bicycle through his neighborhood, he heard the notes of Elvis Presley's "Heartbreak Hotel" coming from a house window. He credits this moment as the one in which he realized Rock 'n' Roll was his destiny. He decided to learn to play the guitar and, in 1956, he managed to persuade his father to buy him one.

At times, in order for destiny to take its course, it needs a bit of a push. In this case, the push was Ivan Vaughan, a friend of Lennon's and a schoolmate of McCartney's (with whom he shared the same birth date). Vaughan played the bass guitar semi-regularly with the Quarrymen and, noting Paul's passion for music, thought that he and John should meet. They met on July 6th, 1957, when the Quarrymen were performing in the garden across from St. Peter's Church in the Liverpool suburb of Woolton. Vaughan brought Paul with him so that John could listen to him play an interpretation of Eddie Cochran's "Twenty Flight Rock" on his guitar. Nothing spectacular

The beginning of the
BEATLES' STORY

happened that day, but John was impressed. This first meeting soon developed into a strong friendship. The following day, on July 7th, 1957, Lennon was convinced of Paul's talent and asked him to join the Quarrymen, which consisted of guitarist Eric Griffiths, Colin Hanton on the drums, Rod Davis on the banjo, Pete Shotton on the washboard, and Len Garry on the bass. The bass was really a 'tea-chest bass' rigged together from a broomstick, a string to be plucked, and a tea chest positioned as a resonator. This was enough for the band to play skiffle and dream of bigger things.

The Quarrymen had their first real gig at the Cavern Club on August 7th, 1957. Paul McCartney didn't perform with them because he was with his brother Mike at a Boy Scout camp in Derbyshire. His official debut with the band took place on October 18th, 1957.

The early days of the Quarrymen group was rather volatile, as there was a constant turnover of members throughout 1958. In February, Paul tried to establish order by convincing John to listen to a young guitarist friend of his who, according to McCartney, possessed real talent. This was of course George Harrison. John listened to him play and thought he was very good, but he believed George was too young (George was only fifteen years old at the time). Paul insisted and went as far as to organize another audition. While seated on the upper floor of a double-decker bus driving through Liverpool, Paul and John listened to George play Bill Justis's "Raunchy," a hit that had been released a few months earlier. This erased John's doubts and he accepted George into the Quarrymen as the group's guitar soloist. The three met frequently, playing together whenever they could. They went to John's or Paul's house after school to practice, writing their first songs in these humble places and playing them for family and friends. They still had a long

19 George Harrison, John Lennon, and Paul McCartney in front of Paul's house in 1960. Ringo Starr joined the band two years later.

way to go, but the group felt a special connection and confidence that they hoped would carry them far.

After some initial hesitation, they decided to record their first single on July 12th, 1958, at the Phillips' Sound Recording Service in Liverpool. The band consisted of John, Paul, George, Colin Hanton, and pianist John "Duff" Lowe, who was hired because of his ability to play arpeggios. By now they were rehearsing frequently at Paul's house on Forthlin Road. In the studio that day, they recorded "That'll Be the Day" by Buddy Holly and "In Spite of All the Danger," an original piece written by McCartney and Harrison. Only one record was pressed, and the first stone of the Beatles cathedral shifted into place. The songs weren't released until 1995, in the *Anthology 1* collection. The original copy of the recording is now owned by McCartney.

Three days later, on July 15th, 1958, John's mother Julia died after being hit by an automobile a few steps from her sister Mimi's house on Menlove Avenue. This was a traumatic experience for John, who found that playing music was the only thing he could do to try to heal the wound.

The Quarrymen continued to perform. John was the leader, and Paul was the ideal partner. They found a club, the Casbah, which hired them to perform each Saturday evening for a period of seven weeks. Consequently, for seven evenings, until October 10th, 1959, the band had four members—John, Paul, George, and Ken Brown—though they still didn't have a regular drummer, as they couldn't find a good replacement for Colin Hanton, who had left the group in January. Ken decided to leave the band after the last evening at the Casbah, so the future of the Quarrymen began to look bleak. After all this time, it was still just the same trio of Lennon, McCartney, and Harrison.

They settled on a new name for themselves: Johnny & The

1959

Moondogs. Their musical talents improved rapidly, and by now the trio had developed a small following of dedicated fans who would show up at clubs to watch them play. They also participated in competitions, playing in the regional final of the *Carroll Levis TV Star Search* in Manchester. Everything was beginning to fall into place, and the history of the Beatles was about to begin.

2

1960-1961
THE BAND IS BORN

THE INTENSE RHYTHM
OF ROCK 'N' ROLL
IN THE HAMBURG CLUBS

On January 17th, 1960, Stuart Fergusson Victor Sutcliffe, a student at the Liverpool College of Art and a close friend of John Lennon's, sold one of his paintings, titled *Summer Painting*, to the Walker Art Gallery in Liverpool. It was purchased by Sir John Moores in person, a well-known philanthropist who, three years earlier, had established an art prize worth 65 pounds—a considerable sum at the time. The same age as John, Stu Sutcliffe was born in Edinburgh in June of 1940 and was a promising artist who painted and drew masterfully. He lived with John in a small apartment in Gambier Terrace. Handsome and personable, he also had a certain flair for musical performances. He could sing well and played a bit of piano and guitar. While at a table in the Casbah Coffee Club, Paul and John persuaded him to spend the prize money on a Hofner bass guitar rather than on canvases and colors. He had never played a bass in his life,

WITH 'STU' SUTCLIFFE,
THE FIFTH BEATLE,
THE BAND IS READY FOR HAMBURG

but he finally relented and became the band's bassist. The group had another new member! But what should they call themselves now? Stu proposed The Beatles, which they used for a little while. They still didn't have a regular drummer; Paul's brother Mike was a temporary solution. He played percussion and beat time with whatever drum-like instrument he could find.

They changed their name again, to the Silver Beetles, enlisting drummer Tommy Moore. This was the name they used for auditions organized on May 10th, 1960 by the manager of Billy Fury (Liverpool's first rock star). The auditions were meant to find a young backing band for Fury's tour. Unfortunately, Tommy Moore didn't show up at the Blue Angel, the club belonging to the Silver Beetles' new manager Allan Williams. He was quickly replaced by Johnny Hutchinson, the drummer of the band Cass and the Cassanovas. The audition proved unsuccessful, but the band made a good impression, and on May 18th, they were hired as the backing band for Johnny Gentle's upcoming tour of Scotland. Before the tour, the band played another concert in Liverpool on May 14th. This time, they chose the name the Silver Beats, which they dropped immediatley after this single performance. For the tour, Tommy Moore was once again selected as the group's drummer. The performances went well, but the relationship between Lennon and Moore deteriorated, and by mid-June, the drummer had left the band again. He was replaced by Norman Chapman, who played with the Silver Beetles for only three weeks. Other drummers were hired, but none of them seemed to fit with the rest of the band. For one concert, they even decided to let Paul play the drums!

Then came a crucial turning point: the band was offered a chance to play clubs in Hamburg, Germany. This was a great opportunity to make some money and build an international fan base. The problem was that the Beetles (or Silver Beatles, as they often called themselves) were still in need of a good drummer. George told the other members that the son of Mona Best, the owner of the Casbah club, played the drums and that his mother had just given him a brand-new drum kit. On August 12th, 1960, they went to the club to ask Pete Best to join the band.

Randolph Peter Best was born on November 24th, 1941. He loved to play music, was popular with the ladies, and he had organized his own band, the Blackjacks, after the Quarrymen were no longer the permanent band in his mother's club. He did well in school and had no problems finding a job, but when the Silver Beetles asked him to go to Hamburg with them to perform, he was ecstatic. The word 'Silver' was eliminated from the band name, and with Pete Best on the drums, the Beatles were officially born.

The official date for the debut of the quintet, consisting of John, Paul, George, Stu, and Pete, was August 17th, 1960, when they performed at the Indra Club in Hamburg. This was the first of 48 evenings in which they were the main attraction, performing five sets each day, five days a week, and six sets on Saturdays and Sundays, with each set lasting about an hour. They slept together in an old storeroom in a movie theater in town, ate very little, drank a lot, and took a lot of amphetamines to stay awake. But those long hours on the primitive stage of the Indra turned out to be a fantastic apprenticeship for the band. They played whatever they wanted, attempting to satisfy and charm the audiences of rowdy Germans. Slowy, through trial and error, they put together a steady repertoire of songs. They learned how to act on the stage and how to fire up the crowd. They also learned how to enjoy themselves despite playing the same songs night after night. In short, they became a true band, mastering all the skills

24 A poster announcing the concerts of the Beatles and Rory Storm at the Kaiserkeller in Hamburg in 1960.

24-25 The Beatles at the Hamburg Fun Fair. From left to right, Pete Best, George Harrison, John Lennon, Paul McCartney, and Stuart Sutcliffe. (Photograph by: Astrid Kirchherr.)

it takes to build a career in the music industry. The Indra performances ended earlier than planned, on October 3rd, as many of the Indra's neighbors complained about the noise the club produced every night. So the Beatles moved on to the Kaiserkeller, a bigger club with a real stage that could accommodate a much large audience. On October 4th, they began a series of 56 nights at the club, which was on the same street (the Große Freiheit) as the Indra. The audiences were typically made up of sailors, gangsters, prostitutes, drunks, young people, and passersby, and the band shared the evening concerts with another Liverpool group, Rory Storm and the Hurricanes, which had an excellent drummer by the name of Ringo Starr.

26 The Beatles during their first series of concerts in Hamburg in 1960, when they backed Tony Sheridan.

26-27 February 1961: The Beatles onstage at the Cavern Club in Liverpool.

They got a chance to play with Ringo on October 15th, 1960, to record a song with Lu Walters, the Hurricanes' bassist. The Beatles began to feel at home in this singular, chaotic environment. The band enjoyed Hamburg, particularly Stu Sutcliffe, who had met a girl named Astrid Kirchherr with whom he had fallen in love with. Astrid was the person who persuaded him to acquire a more distinguished Rock 'n' Roll look, with longer hair and a cooler attitude. And Hamburg loved the Beatles—so much that a competitor of the Kaiserkeller, the Top Ten Club, which had better equipment and tended to attract politer audiences, offered the band a contract. But on November 20th, 1960, during one of the frequent police raids of bars and clubs at that time, officers discovered that George was a minor. He was only seventeen and couldn't perform in a nightclub meant for adults only. To make matters worse, he didn't have a real work permit. George was sent back to Liverpool the following day. Frantically, in a single night, he taught John all of his guitar parts, and the Beatles stayed in Hamburg, playing at the Kaiserkeller for a few evenings without George while waiting to move to the Top Ten Club.

Now only Paul and Pete slept in the backstage area of the Bambi Kino cinema, as John and Stu had moved to a room above the new club. On the evening of November 29th, Paul and Pete began gathering up their belongings to join the other members of the band. There wasn't enough light in the small room to see what they were doing, so they decided to burn something; this caused a small fire, which they immediately put out. But the movie theater owner was furious and called the police. The two were accused of arson and arrested, and the next day they were deported back home to Liverpool.

John decided to stay in Hamburg for a while with Stu, who in the meantime had moved into Astrid's home. For a moment, this seemed to be the end of the band. Lennon tried to play music with other people to earn money, but it didn't work out, and he returned to Liverpool after only ten days to join the others, waiting a week before telling them he was back. In the meantime, Pete had returned to the Casbah, Paul had found a job in a factory, and Harrison was waiting to play music again. The group drifted together again without Stu, resuming their engagements at the Casbah, where Chas Newby of the Blackjacks filled in on bass for four concerts. The men had changed during their stint in Hamburg, and their professionalism and stage presence began to attract larger audiences. However, the group missed Stu on the bass. When he returned from Hamburg, the band fully regained its former equilibrium. They played continuously and made their debut at the Cavern as the Beatles on February 9th, 1961 (previously they had played there as the Quarrymen). This was the first of about 155 appearances for the lunchtime crowd and 125 appearances fo the evening crowd. On April 1st, 1961, the band returned to Hamburg to play at the Top Ten Club, where they stayed until the 1st of July. While in Germany again, they were contacted by Bert Kaempfert, a famous orchestra conductor and an executive at Polydor Records. He wanted them to be the backing band for Tony Sheridan, who was currently making recordings. Without Stu, and with Paul on the bass, the Beatles recorded a few songs with Sheridan, including one written by Lennon and Harrison. "My Bonnie," the single released from those sessions and credited to Tony Sheridan and The Beat Brothers, went to fifth place on the German charts. But this success didn't last long. In August of

1961, Stu told the group that he wanted to leave the band to live with Astrid Kirchherr and continue his art studies. Paul borrowed his bass guitar and officially became the bassist. Now there were only four Beatles.

They became a close-knit group with excellent onstage chemistry that allowed them to make the audience go wild. Their repertoire at this time consisted of Rock 'n' Roll, pop, and soul, but there was something unique about their approach—they took pop music seriously, treating the melodies and lyrics as though they were playing music in an orchestra. This approach gained popularity with yonger audiences, who began to view it as an alternative to their parents' grim, postwar world. And the Beatles could play everything, from Chuck Berry to Motown, with an energy and style that seemed lacking in other perfomers. Slowly, they also began writing their own songs. This second trip to Hamburg was a success, to say the least, and when the band returned to Liverpool, they found enthusiastic audiences of young people waiting to watch them perform.

Brian Epstein, who ran his parents' NEMS (North End Music Stores) shop in Liverpool, understood this too, but not right away, despite the fact that the shop sold pop records. Things clicked for him when a boy named Raymond Jones walked into NEMS one morning and asked Epstein for a copy of the "My

Now with a manager, BRIAN EPSTEIN, everything's set to go: there's the band, the Cavern club, and the flock of Merseyside teenagers

Bonnie" single. This made Epstein curious, and he went to listen to the band at the Cavern. On December 10th, 1961, he offered to be the band's first official manager.

Things were improving steadily for the Beatles. The band consisted of John, Paul, George, and Pete. They had a manager (Brian Epstein), a regular venue (the Cavern), and a city full of fans (Liverpool). The young people of Liverpool and its surrounding areas were demanding a new type of sound, which became known as the Merseybeat. Liverpool at this time boasted a large number of bands, clubs, and young people; with all this fermenting, conditions were ripe for the birth of a new approach to music. There was even a local newspaper featuring news about upcoming local bands (called the *Mersey Beat*). But the Beatles were much more than a Merseybeat band. They played many covers in many genres and played them well, and Lennon and McCartney had begun an extraordinary collaboration as songwriters. The two were in perfect sync, working in unison to write rock songs that would change the course of popular music. This was the beginning of a revolution that would soon spread to the rest of the world.

3

1962–1965
FROM THE FIRST RECORD
TO TOTAL TRIUMPH

FROM THE CAVERN CLUB
TO THE TOP OF THE WORLD:
THE EXPLOSION OF BEATLEMANIA

The epoch-making day was January 1st, 1962. The Beatles—John, Paul, George, and Pete—went to London for a very important appointment, an audition with Dick Rowe of Decca Records. Mike Smith, a Decca talent scout, had heard them play at the Cavern and had contacted Epstein to set up an appointment, which was about signing a recording contract. The four and Epstein arrived at 165 Broadhurst Gardens, West Hampstead, London, plugged their instruments in the Decca amplification system, and played fifteen songs, including three written by Lennon and McCartney.

The boys were tired after a night of New Year's partying, and the Decca executives arrived late and in a bad mood. Consequently, at the end of an hour-long session, Rowe, having to choose between the Beatles and the Londoners Brian Poole and The Tremeloes, opt-

THEY GO TO LONDON FOR THE AUDITION, BUT RECEIVE A FLAT REFUSAL

ed for the latter and uttered a sentence to Epstein that became famous: "Guitar groups are on their way out, Mr. Epstein." So, no contract for the Beatles and no first record. However, Epstein kept the tapes and took them to HMV on Oxford Street, where he had them pressed onto discs. The studio disc cutter Jim Foy liked the Beatles and suggested that Epstein contact a music publisher, Sid Coleman, of Ardmore & Beechwood, a subsidiary of EMI. Coleman was equally impressed by the Beatles' music and organized an appointment with George Martin, the head of Parlophone. Martin accepted the meeting and made an appointment for February 13th. The meeting was a success. Martin listened to the Decca recordings and, although he wasn't enthusiastic, he saw something special in these four young men from Liverpool.

In the meantime, the band continued to play every day, and soon they became one of the most popular bands in Liverpool. The Cavern was their turf, and everything seemed to be moving along smoothly. They got another new job in Hamburg that was meant to last for two months, starting on April 11th. But when they arrived to the city, they were met with the news that Stu Sutcliffe had died of a cerebral hemorrhage. They were devastated, particularly Lennon.

In the meantime, George Martin had made up his mind and asked Epstein to come to his office. "The songs Epstein had me listen to," Martin recalled in the book *The Beatles' Recording Sessions*, "did not particularly impress me, the songs were not exactly brilliant, but something sounded interesting. 'It's no use listening to these tapes,' I told Epstein. 'I'll meet them in person; take them to the studio.'" Epstein didn't waste any time and immediately sent a telegram to the Beatles, who were still in Hamburg, and organized their trip back to London. The quartet consisted of Paul McCartney, John Lennon, George Harrison, and Pete Best.

Many musicians had auditioned in the EMI studios over the years. Darien Angadi, Jill and The Boulevards, Elaine Truss, and Thomas Wallis and The Long Riders are just a few of the bands that passed over the threshold of the building at 3 Abbey Road in that same period. But for the Beatles, June 6th, 1962 was particularly important. "That big studio with huge white screens above us," McCartney recalls in the same book, "had an interminable stairway, at the end of which was the control room. It was like paradise, where the gods lived, and we were there. God, were we nervous." They recorded four songs, but the original tapes from this session were destroyed (one recording of "Besame Mucho" was found much later, in 1980). George Martin took over the recording session while the Beatles were rehearsing "Love Me Do." Then, when it was over, he called them in for a short meeting, during which he and the technicians gave the band advice about their equipment: "They had such worn-out equipment," said Norman Smith, one of the technicians in the studio that day.

"There was as much noise coming from the amps as there was from the instruments." Yet the session proved to be pivotal, as George Martin decided to sign a contract with the band. He also set a date for a new session: September 4th, 1962. The Beatles would use this session to record their first single. "At that meeting, George took me, George, and John to one side," McCartney recalled, "and said he was really unhappy with the drummer and asked us if we would consider changing him. We were not particularly bonded with Pete, even though we knew him from day one . . . he was always different from us three. So George, John, and I decided to call Ringo."

1962

34 The Beatles performing live in 1962, a short time before signing their first recording contract. From left: George Harrison, John Lennon, Paul McCartney, and drummer Pete Best.

35 A group photograph taken in 1962.

The relationship between the original trio and Pete Best had already deteriorated. The drummer wasn't following the band's style; he liked other kinds of music, and he dressed like a rocker, with a forelock instead of the longer hair the other three had. Additionally, his good looks and success with the girls made the others jealous. On August 16th, 1962, John, Paul, and George allowed Brian Epstein to fire Pete Best. To replace him, they wanted a friend of theirs, Richard Starkey, whose stage name was Ringo Starr. Ringo was the drummer for the band Rory Storm and the Hurricanes. The two bands had performed together in Hamburg. As a result, Ringo was already familiar with most of the Beatles' song repertoire. Ringo accepted the offer and began playing with the band on August 18th, 1962. The famous quartet was now complete. On September 4th, 1962, John, Paul, George, and Ringo went to the EMI studios on Abbey Road to record their first songs.

Richard Henry Starkey was born on July 7th, 1940, in a small, terraced house in Dingle, one of the poorest areas of Liverpool. His childhood was marked by illness. When he was six, he had acute appendicitis and was in a coma for more than two months. At the age of thirteen, he caught pneumonia with complications, which kept him in the hospital for extended stays over a two-year period. Yet it was precisely because he was obliged to stay at home that, with the help of his mother's husband, Harry Graves, he became enamored with music and drumming. The rise of Rock 'n' Roll overwhelmed him, and he joined his first skiffle band in 1957—the Eddie Clayton Skiffle Group. He joined the Darktown Skiffle Group two years later, and then became a member of Al Caldwell's Texans, which soon changed its name to Rory Storm and the Hurricanes. Together with Al Caldwell, who became Rory Storm, Starkey also changed his name, choosing Ringo Starr. The band enjoyed great success in Liverpool, becoming the most popular group. They also played in the same clubs as the Beatles, both in Liverpool and in Hamburg. Ringo got along with everyone in the Beatles, had an amiable, easy-going character, and loved the band's music. When they asked him to join, he didn't hesitate in saying yes.

"We returned to London on September 4th for the recordings of 'Love Me Do'," McCartney stated, "and we found out that Martin didn't like Ringo either. We were really surprised, because for us, Ringo was the best in Liverpool, he'd played with Rory Storm and the Hurricanes, there couldn't be anyone better. And no, there was George Martin who decided to put Andy White at the drums and leave Ringo watching from the sidelines. It was really humiliating for him." The recordings were done early in the morning so that the band could return to Liverpool in the evening. They did fifteen versions of "Love Me Do," written by Lennon and McCartney, and an unspecified number of takes for "How Do You Do It," a song written by Mitch Murray and Barry Manson that Martin wanted to use as the band's first single. But the Beatles resisted. They didn't want that song—they wanted one of their own songs to be the single. Martin said, "I liked 'How Do You Do It' a lot, but when everything is said and done, the boys in the band were right. They wanted to play their own songs, so we chose 'Love Me Do'." But Martin was also right; just after the Beatles rejected the song for a second time, it was used by another Liverpool band, Gerry and The Pacemakers, and it topped the charts.

At the end of the recordings, Martin asked the group to replace Starr in "Love Me Do," and the band returned to the studio on September 11th to make new recordings, this time with Andy White at the drums. That same day, they also recorded "P.S. I Love You" and "Please Please Me." The former was chosen as the B-side for the single. On October 2nd, George Martin had the Beatles sign a five-year contract with Parlophone, and on October 5th, "Love Me Do" was officially released. The record, in the version with Ringo as the drummer (the one with Andy White would be released on their first album), went to 17th on the English charts on December 27th, 1962, which marked the beginning of an extraordinary musical adventure. "Love Me Do" was a song that they had rewritten and practiced many times; Paul McCartney wrote it one morning in 1958, when he was playing hookey from school (he was only sixteen years old at the time). The song was signed by both Paul and John, respecting an agreement they made at the beginning of their friendship. This agreement of shared authorship and respect was maintained up until the breakup of the band in 1970. Paul sang the song and John played the harmonica, and if you listen to the album version, Ringo's touch can also be heard, even though he was only playing the tambourine.

LOVE ME DO, THE BEATLES' FIRST SINGLE, IS RELEASED ON OCTOBER 5TH, 1962

36 *One of the first photos of the band after Ringo Starr became their drummer, here seen at the Liverpool harbor.*

AT FIRST NOTHING HAPPENS; THE BEATLES RESUME THEIR HABITUAL LIFESTYLE AND THE SHOWS IN HAMBURG

During this period, the Beatles' former life and routine remained largely same: concerts at the Cavern for the lunchtime and evening crowds; concerts in provincial Great Britain and in many of the suburbs of Liverpool. Their audiences slowly grew, and the band became increasingly close-knit and dependent on each other; the arrival of Ringo had completed the picture, and it wasn't long before he was given the chance to contribute backing vocals to some of the band's songs. They went back to Hamburg once again to perform in fourteen concerts, had their first audition with British TV (which was unsuccessful), played again at the Cavern, where George Martin first saw them perform live, and then finished the year by returning to Hamburg for the last time. The year 1962 was another beginning for the band, as one of their new singles was about to transform their lives.

38-39 A 1962 portrait of the quartet. From left to right: Ringo Starr, George Harrison, John Lennon with the harmonica, and Paul McCartney.

1963

On January 11th, 1963, the single "Please, Please Me" was released, and this time the Beatles immediately soared to no. 1 on the English charts. This was the beginning of a cultural revolution, as the Beatles' model of a band was very different from the current model. First and foremost, they had a collective name, meaning the band wasn't an orchestra or a group accompanying a famous frontman. In fact, they didn't even have a real frontman; John, Paul, and George all performed in front of the audience. Ringo was of course behind them, but this was only for technical reasons. All of them sang, alternating the lead for different songs, and no one hogged the spotlight, although John, the most charismatic

THEY DRESS ALIKE, ALL FOUR SING, AND THERE IS NO LEADER: THEY ARE A UNIT

and boldest member of the band, was certainly the one who stood out the most. For performances, the group tended to wear the same clothes, as if to say, "there's no difference between any of us." They all had long hair. Of course, it was much shorter than certain styles of men's hair today, but at the time it was considered long. All of them were cheerful, entertaining, and amiably provocative; they exuded charm, sensuality, energy, and a sense of collectiveness that young people at the time wanted to see onstage. They were quite young themselves, and it seemed like they had no desire whatsoever to grow old. Their performances were orderly and professional, like seasoned entertainers, but at the same time, they communicated a spontaneity and directness that seemed alien to the music their parents listened to. In short, the sound they created was like a bell for the boys and girls of England to emerge from the drabness of the postwar period and begin painting the world in bright new colors.

40-41 The four young Beatles smiling for a photographer in 1962. They almost seem to be wearing uniforms.

Medley and Russell. It was a mixture of pop, Rock 'n' Roll, and soul, all translated, recast, and recalibrated in the new style that was born in Merseyside, in the heart of Liverpool, at the Cavern Club. In fact, George Martin would have preferred to cut the album at the Cavern; that was the original plan, in order to capture the live energy of the band, but he ultimately decided in favor of a slightly more polished sound.

On February 11th, 1963, the Beatles recorded their first album, *Please, Please Me*. Yes, that's right—on February 11th, in only one day—or, to be more precise, in nine hours and 45 minutes, during three three-hour sessions in the Abbey Road studios and under the attentive leadership of George Martin. In less than ten hours, in a single day, the history of pop music changed direction thanks to fourteen songs—eight by the Lennon-McCartney duo and six covers by other artists including Arthur Alexander, Goffin and King, Burt Bacharach, Luther Dixon, Scott and Marlow, and

In only one day (February 11th, 1963), in three sessions lasting 9 hours and 45 minutes, the Beatles recorded their debut album, *Please Please Me*.

With the exception of "Twist & Shout," it wasn't the covers that sent the Beatles to the top of the charts. This feat was thanks to the songs that Paul and John wrote, as well as the overall sound and image of the band. These elements, taken as a whole, made the Beatles' approach seem new and revolutionary. This first album was released in March, and the band immediately began a tour. They remained at the top of the charts for 29 weeks straight. What only a few loyal fans had seen on the first two singles now became clear to everyone. The music that, until then, had echoed exclusively in the small Casbah Club and the Cavern Club in Liverpool, was now ringing in the ears of an entire generation of English teens, and it was soon on its way to conquering the rest of the world.

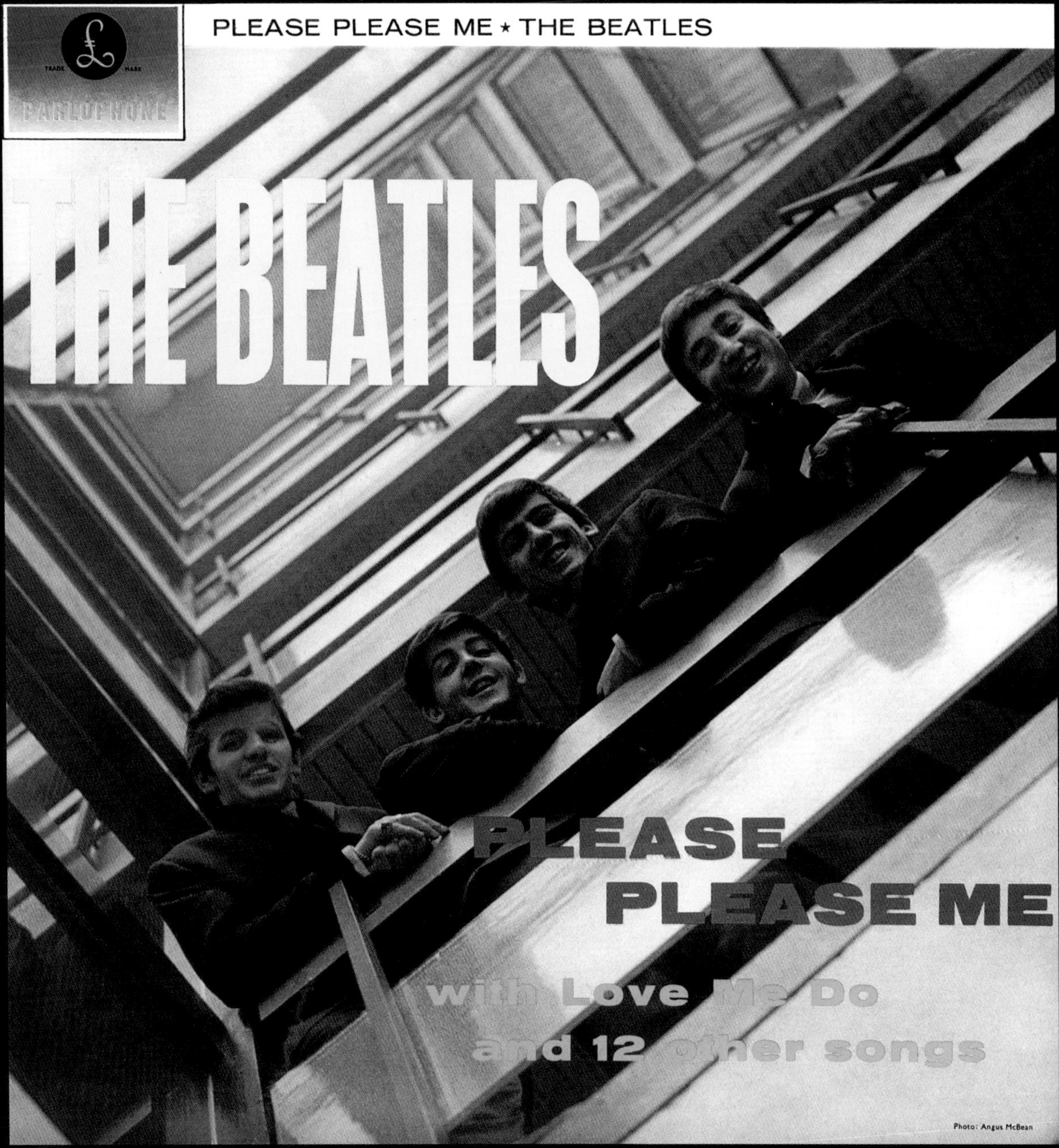
PLEASE PLEASE ME ★ THE BEATLES
TRADE MARK
PARLOPHONE
THE BEATLES
PLEASE
PLEASE ME
with Love Me Do
and 12 other songs
Photo: Angus McBean

It's impossible not to be moved by the opening song of the album, "I Saw Her Standing There." But "Love Me Do," "P.S. I Love You," and the title song of the album, "Please, Please Me," also sparked great enthusiasm. The record contained something for everyone: Elvis's Rock 'n' Roll, the rhythm of soul music, and the art of pop. But above all, it held the dreams of four youngsters born at the end of the war who were finally fulfilling their destinies. Lennon and McCartney had proven they could translate the passions of their generation into lighthearted, immediate, and original songs, with "a bit of help from their friends." On the album, George sang "Chains" and "Do You Want to Know a Secret," and Ringo sang the song "Boys." The recording of the album cost 400 pounds, and each of the four received the union wage of £21.50 for their nine hours work. The future of rock would never be the same.

The recording of the album cost 400 pounds, and each of the four received the union wage of £21.50 for their nine hours of work. The future of rock would never be the same.

Before the album was released, the Beatles returned to the studio on March 5th, 1963 to record their third single, "From Me to You." In fact, Martin and Epstein decided that the band would record and release four new singles and two albums every year. This was less challenging than it sounds, as the band already had an extraordinary repertoire of covers that they had experimented with and polished during their long years playing music in Liverpool and Hamburg. Additionally, the Lennon and McCartney composition machine was by now in perfect working order. Around this time, while they were on tour with Helen Shapiro, they wrote "From Me to You" only five days before the song had to be recorded.

Everything began to change. On March 9th, they began their second tour of England. On March 22nd, their debut album was released, and only fifteen days later, it reached the 'silver disc' mark for selling more than 250,000 copies. On April 13th, they made their first appearance on national TV (BBC).

44-45 The Beatles and George Martin with the silver disc they were awarded for having sold 250,000 copies of the album Please Please Me.

Their personal lives were also changing. A few months earlier, on August 23rd, 1962, John had secretly married Cynthia Powell. He had met her in art school and had maintained a relationship with her since 1958. Lennon's son Julian was born on April 8th, 1963. But due to the band's success, it was becoming harder for John to spend time at home in Liverpool. After a concert in London, Paul met the woman who would become his muse and partner for some time: Jane Asher.

Despite the band's meteoric success, there was still something missing—that final leap that would cement the band's reputation as being uniquely tuned to the hopes and struggles of an entire generation. What was missing was a touch of magic made up of notes and words, a song that could explain to the whole world that music was about to evolve. This touch of magic emerged over a two-day period; first in a hotel room in Newcastle, on June 27th, and then in Paul's home on Forthlin Road the following day.

"We sat there one evening, just beavering away while my dad was watching TV and smoking his Player cigarettes, and while we were writing 'She Loves You'," McCartney related. "We actually finished it there because we'd started it in a hotel room. We went into the living room. 'Dad, listen to this. What do you think?' I said. So we played it to him and he said,

'That's very nice, son. But there's enough of this Americanism around. Couldn't you sing *She loves you. Yes! Yes! Yes!*' At which we collapsed into a heap and said, 'No Dad, you don't quite get it.'" Paul's account is a fine example of exactly what was about to occur, that is, the new generation's sound and language was about to dominate the radio, while their parents' generation simply didn't grasp what was happening. The three most important words in the song are 'yeah yeah yeah'. They're not a form of 'Americanism', but rather a code, or a signal. All the teenagers who listened to "She Loves You" simply loved that 'yeah yeah yeah'; they knew what it meant and what was hidden beneath. "She Loves You" was recorded on July 1st, 1963, and it was released on August 23rd. The song "I'll Get You" was added to the other side of the record. The single exploded in popularity, with 1,890,000 copies sold—the largest number of copies of a single sold in history. This record held until 1977, when McCartney himself broke it with one of his solo singles. The song went to the charts on August 31st and stayed there for 31 consecutive weeks; 18 of those weeks were spent within the first three positions. It became no. 1 on September 14th, 1963 and remained here for six weeks, which was enough to make the Beatles the most famous band in the United Kingdom.

47 The Fab Four during one of the recording sessions in the Abbey Road studios in London. In the foreground is George Harrison. John Lennon is seated in front of him, Paul McCartney is standing, and in the background is Ringo Starr.

In the meantime, the four had already begun preparing their second album, recording from mid-July and through the following months, when they weren't performing, touring, or making appearances on TV and radio. They released several EPs with songs from their singles, all of which promptly continued to rise on the charts. The band had real momentum now. The Liverpool period ended on August 3rd, 1963, when the Beatles—along with the Merseybeats, The Escorts, The Roadrunners,

THE LAST CAVERN CONCERT WAS ON AUGUST 3RD, 1963. THE CLUB WAS TOO SMALL FOR THE SUCCESS OF THE BAND

The Sapphires, and Johnny Ringo & The Colts—played for the last time at the Cavern, which had become too small to contain their success.

For the first time in years, they enjoyed a brief vacation in late September. George went to the United States with his sister Louise. John and Cynthia went to Paris, while Paul and Ringo decided to spend time by the sea in Greece. When they all returned home, they immediately went to the studio to record the second album. They also had to prepare for their debut on *Ready, Steady, Go!*, the BBC's most important music program.

48-49 July 18th, 1963, a group photograph of the Liverpool bands managed by Brian Epstein (seen at the far right): The Beatles, Gerry and The Pacemakers, and Billy J Kramer & The Dakotas.

The Beatles's fame had grown enormously in only a few weeks, but the exact birth date normally assigned to Beatlemania is October 13th, 1963, when the band performed at the London Palladium. This concert launched them into the firmament of stardom and attracted the attention of the national media, which began to use the term Beatlemania as a synonym for the burgeoning revolution of this younger generation. The *Sunday Night at the London Palladium* program was a sort of variety show held in a theater but broadcasted on television. It was extremely popular, regularly reaching an audience of millions. The Beatles were

With the London Palladium success, the Beatles became
"THE FABULOUS FOUR"

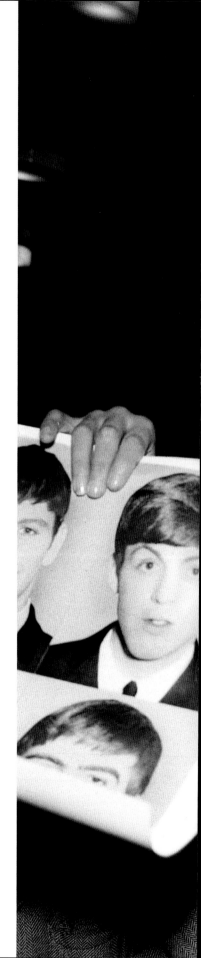

the last band to perform that night, and just before their finale, they were swallowed up by screams from the girls in the audience as they began to play "Twist and Shout." From that moment on, every show and every concert was accompanied by the same hysteria and shrieking on the part of young girls. This younger generation began identifying itself with these four musicians in their twenties who had stormed the stage with a lethal dose of likeableness. The following day, the front page of the newspapers featured the squealing and frenzy of their fans, transforming the Beatles into a phenomenon.

50 *The Fabulous Four onstage in the Palladium of London before an audience of 2,000 screaming fans.*

50-51 *Teenage fans of the Beatles at the ABC Theatre in Plymouth on November 13th, 1963.*

with
the
beatles

PARLOPHONE

On October 17th, they recorded the new single, "I Want to Hold Your Hand," which was released a little more than a month later. A few days earlier, on November 22nd, their second album, *With the Beatles*, was released. Four months had passed since the release of the preceding album, and the situation was quite different—the new album was eagerly awaited by legions of young people throughout the United Kingdom. This same crowd ensured that the album went to the top of the charts immediatley, where it remained for 21 consecutive weeks. It even surpassed their first album, *Please, Please Me*, meaning that the Bealtes had held the top spot on the charts for nearly a year.

The progress made by Lennon and McCartney as songwriters was obvious. Amazingly, the duo wrote seven of the songs on the album, including "All My Loving" and "It Won't Be Long." And for the first time, there was a song written by George: "Don't Bother Me." The other six songs on the album were covers drawn from Rhythm 'n' Blues, soul, and Rock 'n' Roll songs that the band interpreted in their very own fashion. These covers have such a unique sound that people often assume they were written by the Beatles. The image on the cover serves as a contrast to the contents of the album. The songs are brimming with color and cheerfulness,

52 *The cover of* With the Beatles, *the band's second album, released on November 22nd, 1963.*

53 *The cover of the American version of* Meet the Beatles, *the first album of the band published by Capitol Records (January 20th, 1964).*

while the cover is a series of black-and-white photographs taken by Robert Freeman. The photos are pasted together, with each member facing the camera in a serious, unsmiling pose; indeed, the band looks almost gloomy. The existential mood of the cover helped separate the Beatles from the rest of the pop world. In the photo, the Beatles appear to be saying, "We're playful but serious." The teenagers who chose to be 'on the side of the Beatles' were well aware of this. And they were 'with the Beatles' in every way possible, through albums, newspapers, posters, and even books. *The Beatles Book*, which was launched by the publisher of *Pop Weekly* and *Beat Instrumental Monthly*, sold 350,000 copies in only a few weeks. Beatlemania became an irrepressible fever that exploded in the early sixties, especially at their live performances.

THE PROGRESS MADE BY LENNON AND MCCARTNEY AS SONGWRITERS WAS OBVIOUS

"Screaming girls launched themselves against the police, sending helmets flying and constables reeling," wrote the *Daily Herald* after the October performance at the London Palladium.

Presented to
PAUL McCARTNEY
by his friends at
E.M.I RECORDS LTD
for the best selling E.P.
AUGUST 1963

On November 29th, the band released their latest single, *I Want to Hold Your Hand*, which was written in the basement of the Asher family home in London. Jane Asher was Paul's girlfriend, and McCartney and Lennon often used the piano in her house to write and rehearse. The day the release was announced, there were half a million order placements for the single, and eventually the requests numbered more than a million, a record for that time. Meanwhile, Epstein established a fan club for the band, and in order to make the members happy, the Beatles sent them their first *Christmas Record*. This tradition continued every year until the group disbanded. The group embarked on their first tour outside England, after which they launched their first tour of the British Isles as headliners.

54-55 *November 18th, 1963: The Beatles show the silver discs presented to them by EMI for their record sales of the LP* Please Please Me, *and "Twist and Shout," the best-selling EP of all time.*

55 *The Beatles performing on TV on the* Thank Your Lucky Stars *show, held in the Alpha Television Studios in the Aston ward of Birmingham on December 15th, 1963.*

56-57 *November 13th, 1963: The Beatles passing through Plymouth in a limousine. John Lennon holds a copy of the* Daily Mirror.

In November of 1963, they were invited to the *Royal Variety Performance*, the most prestigious event of the year. The show always took place before the members of the royal family and was broadcasted on television a few days later. At first the band had doubts about participating, as they didn't like the idea of putting on a show exclusively for establishment types. But Epstein was convinced that the resulting publicity from such a performance would be extremely advantageous for the band in the long run and persuaded them to accept the invitation. Queen Elizabeth didn't attend the show, as she was pregnant with her fourth child, but the royal family was represented by Princess Margaret, her husband Lord Snowdon, and the Queen Mother. The program consisted of 19 performances; the Beatles were the seventh group in line. They began with "From Me to You," followed by "She Loves You" and "'Till There Was You." Then Lennon spoke to the audience: "For our last number, I'd like to ask your help." After a brief pause, he added: "For those of you in the cheap seats, clap your hands; the rest of you can just rattle your jewelry." Walking the tightrope between entertaining and disrespectful, John Lennon won everyone over. For another band, such a performance could easily have resulted in a decline in their popularity and credibility. "They are so fresh and vital. I simply adore them," the Queen Mother declared at the end of the evening. The *Daily Mirror* commented: "If they don't sweep your blues away—brother you're a lost cause. If they don't put a beat in your feet—sister, you're not living." After winning the hearts of the royal family, anything seemed possible. The next step was to conquer the New World.

Epstein spent a lot of time in advance organizing a North American tour for the band. In November, he went to the U.S. to finalize agreements and sign contracts, especially those concerning the band's first appearance on *The Ed Sullivan Show*, scheduled for three consecutive Saturdays in February of 1964. After seeing the response to the Beatles in the United Kingdom, Capitol Records decided to release "I Want to Hold Your Hand" in the U.S. a month early, on December 26th, 1963. By January 18th, the single was in the Top 100, and two weeks later, it was number one on the American charts. On January 20th, Capitol released the band's second album, *Meet the Beatles*, in the U.S. The British Invasion had begun.

58-59 Princess Margaret meets the Beatles backstage after their Royal Variety Performance *of November 4th, 1963, held at the Prince of Wales Theatre in London. The princess attended the show together with the Queen Mother.*

60 The Beatles rehearsing in the afternoon before the Royal Variety Performance at the Prince of Wales Theatre.

60-61 An interesting photograph of the band jumping in unison during their afternoon rehearsal for the Royal Variety Performance (November 4th, 1963).

IN 1963, THE POPULARITY
of the band explodes into
"BEATLEMANIA"

62 Two fans reading the Beatles Fan Club fanzine while waiting to buy their tickets for the concert the band gave on November 23rd, 1963, at Newcastle Upon Tyne.

62-63 Adolescents waiting in the rain in front of the Majestic Ballroom at Birkenhead, hoping to buy tickets for the Beatles' concert.

64 top *Policemen try to restrain overenthusiastic fans in Birmingham, where the band was shooting a performance for the ABC-TV program* Thank Your Lucky Stars.

64 bottom *Fans wait for the Beatles to arrive at the ABC-TV studios in Birmingham.*

65 *Two teenagers screech with enthusiasm during a Beatles concert in Exeter in November 1963.*

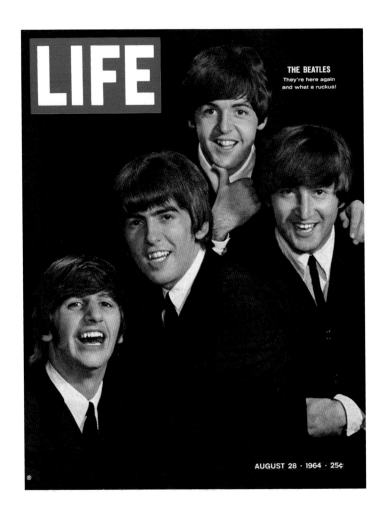

THE BEATLES
They're here again
and what a ruckus!

AUGUST 28 · 1964 · 25¢

NOBODY IS ABLE TO RESIST
the Liverpool band's charm, which
conquers the media world

66 The August 28th, 1964 cover of Life featuring the Beatles, with the line: "They're here again and what a ruckus!"

67 Paul McCartney posing with a Beatles fanzine in 1964. The photo on the back of the magazine is a classic representation of Beatlemania.

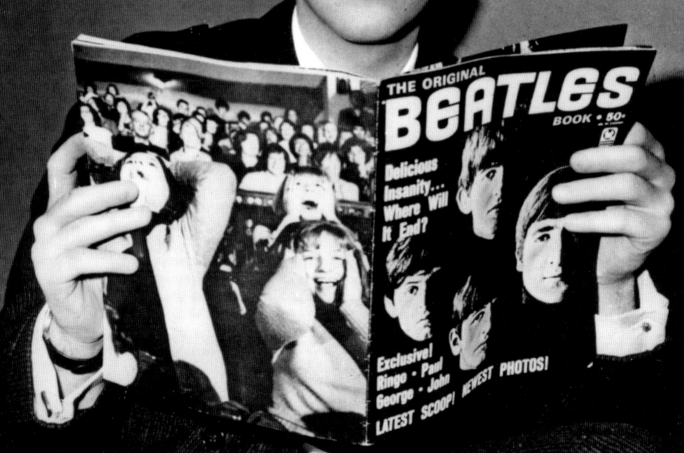

THE BEATLES FAN CLUB
IS BORN IN LIVERPOOL

1964

68 *A fan wearing a delightful hat with images of the Fab Four performing (June 1964).*

69 *February 25th, 1964 was George Harrison's 21st birthday. Here, the secretary of the fan club, Anne Collingham, helps sort out the 52 packages full of birthday greetings.*

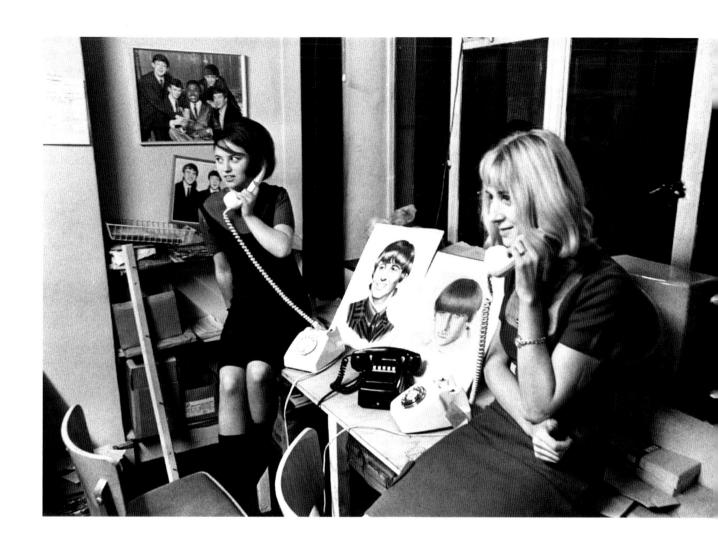

70 The offices of the Beatles Fan Club in a photograph taken on April 10th, 1964. Anne Collingham, 18 years old, and Bettina Rose, 20, were the club's national secretaries.

71 Another photo of the Beatles Fan Club, dating to December 1st, 1964. Anne Collingham, at left, and Bettina Rose are on the phone answering fans' questions about Ringo's health, since the Beatles drummer had temporarily left the band's world tour because of tonsil problems.

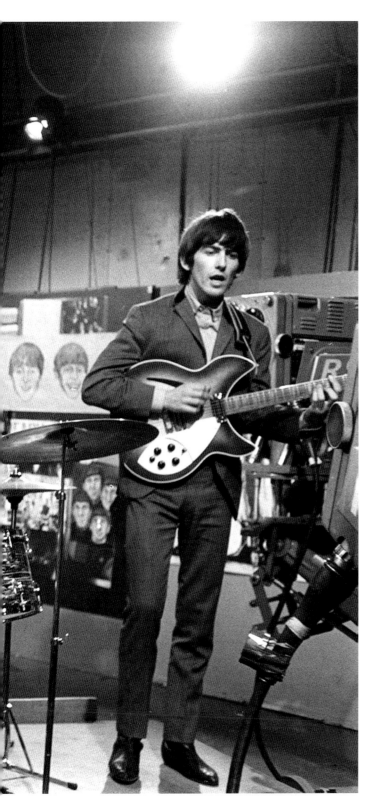

THE EXCITING PERIOD OF "SWINGING LONDON," POP MUSIC, MINISKIRTS, AND BEAT BANDS

74-75 *The Beatles at the Television House of Kingsway during the shooting of the program* Ready, Steady, Go! *(March 20th, 1964). Left to right: Paul, John, Ringo, and George.*

75 *Paul McCartney with his Rickenbacker bass guitar during the shooting of* Ready, Steady, Go!*.*

76-77 Paul McCartney examines his wax double at the Madame Tussauds museum in London.

77 The Beatles sitting in front of their wax statues at Madame Tussauds in April 1964.

The four arrived in New York on February 7th, 1964, and enthusiasm for the band skyrocketed. A large crowd was waiting for the Beatles' arrival at JFK Airport, but the entire nation seemed to be looking forward to hearing them. When they made their debut on *The Ed Sullivan Show* two days later, roughly 73 million Americans tuned in to see what these lads from Liverpool were all about. According to legend, there was actually a national decrease in robberies during their performance, as even the criminals wanted to see the Beatles play.

The Ed Sullivan Show was the lightning before the thunder. In a matter of days, most of teenage America was clamoring for the band's albums, and many boys began asking for haircuts and clothes similar to what the Beatles had sported on TV. America was carried away by the band; no one could resist their power, cheerfulness, and catchy sound. The charts attested to this as well. By the following April, songs by the Beatles occupied the top five spots, while seven of their other songs were among the top thirty. This conquest of the United States took place during the country's mourning period following the death of President Kennedy; the band helped

In April 1964 the Beatles occupied CONTEMPORANEOUSLY the top five spots on the U.S. charts

revive the enthusiasm of young people, who began breaking away from the influence of their parents and families. Young people mobilized in universities and music concerts, envisioning a different lifestyle for themselves. The Beatles were one of the matches to light the fuse, sparking increased interest in rock music and in the music scene in Great Britain. In no time at all, the Rolling Stones, the Kinks, the Dave Clark Five, the Hollies, Petula Clark, The Who, and many other British bands became part of this invasion, dominating popular music for the next few years.

78 The band rehearses before their appearance on The Ed Sullivan Show *(February 8th, 1964).*
On-screen in the foreground is a close-up of McCartney and Harrison.

80-81 *Paul McCartney gives Ed Sullivan pointers on how to play the guitar during the rehearsals of* The Ed Sullivan Show *in the CBS studios in Manhattan.*

THE BEATLES LAND IN NEW YORK, WHICH MARKS THE BEGINNING OF THE INVASION OF THE U.S. ON THE PART OF BRITISH BANDS

82 The Fab Four wave to their fans upon their arrival at JFK airport in New York on
February 7th, 1964.

83 The Beatles answering journalists' questions during the press conference held
immediately after their arrival in New York.

84 John Lennon, Paul McCartney, and Ringo Starr visit Central Park on February 9th, 1964, during the band's first tour in the United States.

85 Ringo, Paul, and John ride through Central Park on one of the traditional horse-drawn cabs during a photograph session.

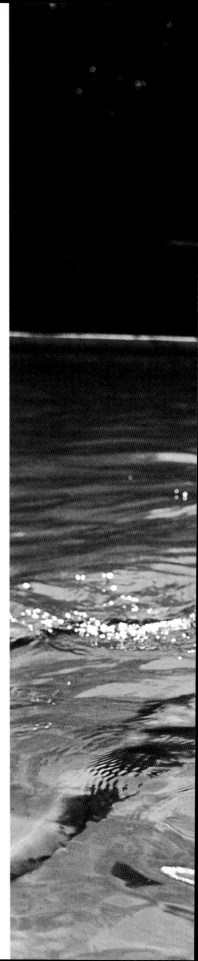

86 The Beatles were in the limelight even when they were trying to relax. Here they enjoy themselves in a pool, to the delight of the Life Magazine photographers.

86-87 Another photograph of the band published in the weekly magazine.

ONLY CASSIUS CLAY
could 'floor' the Beatles at Miami Beach;
a few days later he became world champion

88 On February 18th, 1964, the Beatles met Cassius Clay (who had not yet changed his name to Muhammad Ali).
The future heavyweight champion of the world pretends to floor all four with single punch.

89 The Fab Four 'concede defeat' to Cassius Clay during their merry 1964 meeting.

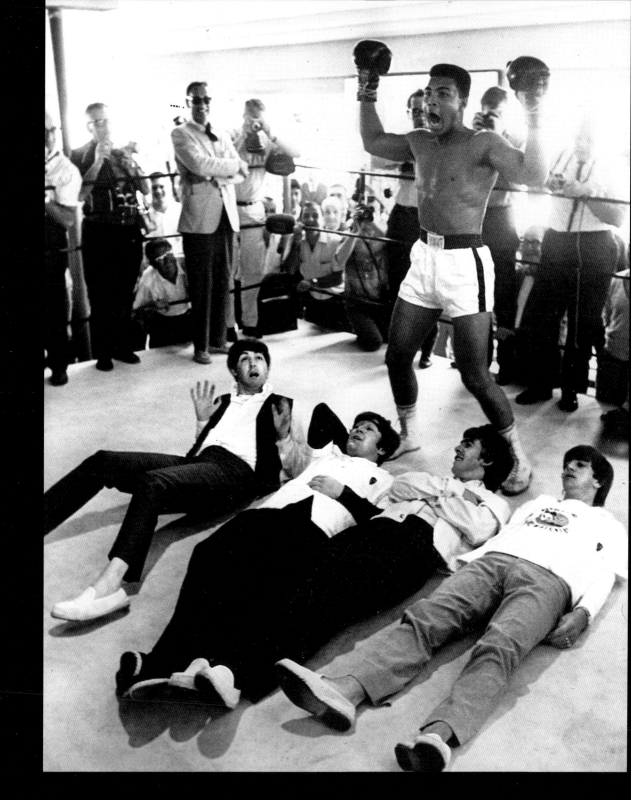

When the Beatles returned to London, the world was at their feet. In March, they began shooting their first movie, the delightful *A Hard Day's Night*, directed by Richard Lester. A few weeks later, Lennon published a book, *In His Own Write*, consisting of stories, poems, and drawings. The filming of the movie lasted almost two months (comprising of 40 working days), and it was during this experience that George met Pattie Boyd, a model who had a walk-on part (another walk-on was the very young Charlotte Rampling). George fell in love with her, and when filming was over at the end of April, he invited her to go on vacation with him. The band was seeking peace and quiet after a hectic period in their lives, and they didn't want the media to know where they were headed. They decided to separate into two groups: John, Cynthia, George, and Pattie went to Tahiti, while Paul, Jane, Ringo, and Maureen went to the Virgin Islands. According to Brian Epstein, in order to keep everything secret, they didn't call one another and created code names for themselves. Paul was Mr. Manning, Ringo was Mr. Stone, Jane was Ms. Ashcroft, and Maureen was Ms. Cockcroft. John was Mr. Leslie, his wife Mrs. Leslie, George Mr. Hargreaves, and Pattie Ms. Bond.

The vacation lasted a little less than four weeks. At the end of May, the band was ready to resume work. By June 4th, they were set to begin their first worldwide tour with their new nickname, the Fabulous Four. They had only a few days to record the songs for their next album, which they did at Abbey Road. After recording, they left for Copenhagen, the first leg of a tour that included 30 performances in Denmark, Holland, Hong Kong, Australia, New Zealand, Sweden, and England. For the first six concerts, they were obliged to replace Ringo, who got a bad case of tonsillitis and laryngitis and was unable to leave with the rest of the band. George Martin suggested calling in a replacement for this first part of the tour, Jimmie Nicol, a recording session artist. As the drummer recalled, he was napping after lunch one day when the telephone rang. It was EMI, and they asked him to go to their studios immediatley for an audition with the Beatles. After two hours of playing for them, they told him to pack his suitcases, as they wanted him to join the band for performances in Denmark. Nicol played with the band for six concerts and one Dutch TV appearance. On June 15, in Melbourne, Ringo returned to reclaim his place behind the drums. Jimmie Nicol had been a Beatle for eleven days.

In June 1964, the film *A Hard Day's Night* was released in British movie theaters

The film *A Hard Day's Night* was released on July 6th, 1964, and was a great success. It was about Beatlemania itself, romanticizing what was really happening to the band during their performances and capturing the hysterics of their fans, their TV appearances, their autograph-signings, and their constant shuttling between hotels and shows. Above all, it emphasized the likeable nature of the four, who played their roles incredibly well. The movie earned Oscar and BAFTA nominations, and many years later, the British Film Institute put it on its list of the 100 best films of the century. Four days after the opening of the film, the band's third album was released, titled *A Hard Day's Night*, naturally.

91 The Beatles running in an alley in London during the shooting of A Hard Day's Night.

92-93 Paul McCartney at Madame Tussauds museum on March 12th, 1964, holding a pair of glass eyes during a break in the shooting of the film A Hard Day's Night.

93 John Lennon and George Harrison joke while holding two pairs of glass eyes, which were part of their wax doubles at Madame Tussauds.

94-95 *The band seen from behind during a scene in* A Hard Day's Night *(1964).*

95 *A pause during the shooting of* A Hard Day's Night. *The Beatles are together with model Pattie Boyd, who later became George Harrison's wife.*

96-97 The band at a rehearsal of one of their recorded performances on The Ed Sullivan Show (February 9th, 1964). Neil Aspinall is next to Paul McCartney, having replaced George Harrison, who wasn't feeling well.

98 *The Beatles on the plane that took them to Liverpool on July 10th, 1964, for the premiere in their hometown of the film* A Hard Day's Night, *directed by Richard Lester.*

98-99 *The band arrives at Liverpool and waves to the fans and photographers waiting for them.*

THE CITIZENS OF LIVERPOOL FILL THE STREETS TO WELCOME THE BAND FOR THE PREMIERE OF *A HARD DAY'S NIGHT*

100-101 Four days after the London premiere, the Beatles arrive in Liverpool to present their first movie, A Hard Day's Night. About 3,000 fans were at the Speke airport to greet them, while another 200,000 persons lined the city streets as the band drove to the cinema.

101 The huge crowd jams the streets of Liverpool to see the Beatles, who had returned to their city.

102-103 The Liverpool police try to restrain the excited fans waiting to see the band ride by.

The Beatles   A Hard Day's Night

also starring
WILFRID BRAMBELL

Produced by
WALTER SHENSON
Directed by
RICHARD LESTER

Screenplay by
ALUN OWEN
Released thru
UNITED ARTISTS

Musical Director
GEORGE MARTIN

SIDE		
ONE	1. A HARD DAY'S NIGHT (VOCAL)	2:28
	2. TELL ME WHY (VOCAL)	2:04
	3. I'LL CRY INSTEAD (VOCAL)	2:06
	4. I SHOULD HAVE KNOWN BETTER (INSTRUMENTAL)	2:16
	5. I'M HAPPY JUST TO DANCE WITH YOU (VOCAL)	1:59
	6. AND I LOVE HER (INSTRUMENTAL)	3:42

SIDE		
TWO	1. I SHOULD HAVE KNOWN BETTER (VOCAL)	2:42
	2. IF I FELL (VOCAL)	2:16
	3. AND I LOVE HER (VOCAL)	2:27
	4. RINGO'S THEME (THIS BOY) (INSTRUMENTAL)	3:06
	5. CAN'T BUY ME LOVE (VOCAL)	2:15
	6. A HARD DAY'S NIGHT (INSTRUMENTAL)	2:00

ALL SONGS WRITTEN BY
LENNON AND McCARTNEY

Produced for disc by George Martin
Recorded in England

Selections contained herein have been previously released by Capitol Records, Inc. or United Artists Records, Inc.

SW-11921

EMI

104 *The back of the cover of* A Hard Day's Night, *which was released in England on July 10th, 1964.*

105 *The cover of* A Hard Day's Night, *designed by Robert Freeman.*

106 Another version of the cover for the soundtrack of A Hard Day's Night, released in 1964.

107 John Lennon at the euphonium (or tenor tuba) deafens Ringo Starr's ears at the Odeon Cinema in Liverpool, at the city's premiere of A Hard Day's Night.

THE BEATLES

oraz dwanaście najnowszych piosenek
w ich pierwszej, pełnej przygód i muzyki komedii

reżyseria Richard Lester

Produkcja Walter Shenson
— United Artists 1964

The Beatles had matured to a remarkable degree and had become far more successful than they could have ever hoped for. There were no more charts to top, no more countries to conquer, and their shows and albums had already earned them enough money to ensure they wouldn't have to work another day in their lives. The only thing left was the music, which was about to change again.

While they were in America, George bought a 12-string Rickenbacker guitar, the second one ever produced, and played it continuously. John became obsessed with the album *The Freewheelin' Bob Dylan* by Bob Dylan. Paul fell in love with Jamaican music. Collectively, the band felt that their approach had become stale. Whatever they released seemed destined for success. This was demonstrated by the release of their single "Can't Buy Me Love," which soon topped the charts and sold 3 million copies through purchase orders alone. All four had acquired more creative power on their albums, which changed the equilibrium between Lennon and McCartney

A Hard Day's Night opens with a magical single chord that is there only to lend A TOUCH OF PURE ART

even though the songs were technically attributed to both of them. "Most of the singles were mine," Lennon declared in 1980, "but the others had a lot of wonderful ideas." A single chord seemed to symbolize the band's changing tastes: the one at the beginning of the song "A Hard Day's Night." It's a complex chord, strident and magical (and totally useless within the context of the song). In fact, it immediately disappears from the track and is never heard again. But this chord was a slight artistic touch that signaled the start of a more creative approach. For the first time during the Beatles' adventure, they weren't just focused on success. They had begun dedicating themselves to art and playing music to express something deeper.

108 A Polish poster advertising the movie A Hard Day's Night.

There are songs on *A Hard Day's Night* that break the formulaic rules of catchy pop, such as "If I Fell" or the beautiful "And I Love Her." These are of course paired with catchy classics like "Can't Buy Me Love" and "You Can't Do That." But on this album, there were no covers, only Beatles songs. Whatever their direction going forward, the band knew it wanted to write more of its

BEATLES FOR SALE WAS THE TITLE OF THE NEW ALBUM, RELEASED IN DECEMBER 1964

own music. Their instincts had changed, and it soon became clear that they weren't content to remain a tennage heartthrob band forever, especially John, who had written most of the songs for *A Hard Day's Night*.

In August 1964, the band returned to America to play a few shows. In New York, they spent time with Bob Dylan. According to legend, Dylan got the four and Brian Epstein to smoke marijuana for the first time. The tour, which began on August 19th, ended on September 20th, and the Beatles went back to England the following day.

Only two months after *A Hard Day's Night* was released, the band was in the studio again to begin recording a new album. Once again, the recording work was slotted between media appearances, concerts, and radio and television shows. This didn't leave much time for writing original material, so the band once again decided to include songs from their extensive repertoire of covers and from the compositions Lennon and McCartney had worked on during the Hamburg years. *Beatles for Sale* was the title of the new album, released in December of 1964. It had six covers in total. The original songs included "Baby's in Black," dedicated to Astrid Kirchner, "Eight Days A Week," "What You're Doing," and "I Don't Want to Spoil the Party." Paul wrote the song "Every Little Thing" and pushed for the inclusion of "I'll Follow the Sun," which he had written years ago. Lennon wrote "No Reply" and "I'm a Loser." The track "Eight Days a Week" opens with a fade-in, the first time such a technique was used on a pop studio recording. Lennon openly admitted to having been influenced by Bob Dylan, and McCartney mined his adolescence for the stories threaded into the songs he wrote.

111 *The Beatles pose in front of the American flag in April 1964, in one of the photos used to promote their first U.S. tour, which began in August 1964. Their 32 shows covered 24 cities in 34 days.*

112 Delirious fans wait for the Beatles in front of the Forest Hills Tennis Stadium in New York before the band's concert on August 28th, 1964.

THE SCREAMING OF THE FANS BECAME THE ENDLESS SOUNDTRACK OF THE BAND'S TOURS AND SHOWS

113 Fans waiting outside the Delmonico Hotel in New York, where the band stayed before their Forest Hills Tennis Stadium concert.

114 *George Harrison in the Marquee Studios in London, recording the band's Christmas greeting message to the members of the Beatles Fan Club (October 10th, 1965).*

1 9 6 5

The year 1965 began with *Beatles for Sale* still holding the number one spot on the charts. The four thus decided to treat themselves to another vacation. In February, there was a second wedding, this time between Ringo Starr and Maureen Cox, a girl from Liverpool he had met at the Cavern Club and to whom he had been engaged for quite some time. That same month, the band recorded a large number of songs. The general atmosphere was one of happiness and harmony, and this period is regarded as one of the most productive in the band's history. The influence of Bob Dylan's music led John to compose in a more personal manner. Paul became enamored with avant-garde composers, and George discovered the sitar. These new interests would lead to richer, more complex and fascinating songs that helped push the boundaries of pop. By 1965, many bands were doing the same. Bob Dylan, for example, was constantly reinventing himself. At the Newport Folk Festival in 1965, he generated controversy among folk purists for his sudden use of electric instruments. There were the Rolling Stones, who recorded the song "Satisfaction" in 1965, a manifesto of the young who rejected the lifestyle and commercialism of their parents. Even more outspoken was The Who, who frequently loved to destroy their instruments onstage. They recorded their rock anthem "My Generation" in 1965. The Beatles were certainly not a band to be outdone. Before they could write new music, they had to respect a film commitment they had previously agreed to. The band spent many weeks working on their second feature film, *Help!*. This film wasn't received quite as well by critics as *A Hard Day's Night* was, but it was still a hit.

Rock was born in 1965, with the Rolling Stones' "Satisfaction," The Who's "My Generation," and Bob Dylan's first electric concert in Newport, Rhode Island.

A new single, "Ticket to Ride," was released on April 9th, and it was obvious now that the Beatles had begun to apply themselves more seriously to their recording work. They now understood that, at Abbey Road, they no longer needed to merely replicate the songs they could play live. With the help of the invaluable George Martin, they could now try to broaden the field and experiment with different sounds, harmonies, and instruments. "Ticket to Ride" was the first example of a new, more open style. In the weeks that followed, their commitments overlapped—the band was trying to record a new album, their mornings were spent shooting the new movie, and their afternoons and evenings were reserved for radio and TV appearances.

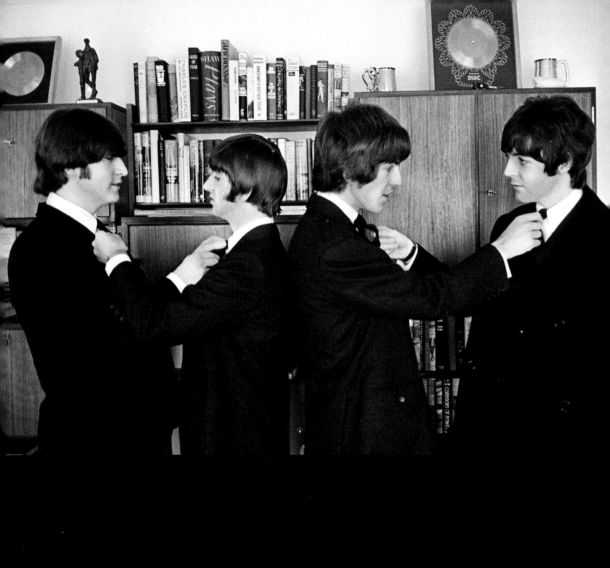

In June, the announcement came that the Beatles were nominated to be Members of the British Empire, a major honor offered by the royal family itself. The four became baronets, the reason being that they had contributed to and strengthened the cultural heritage of England. Thanks in part to the Beatles, London became *swinging London*, a mecca for young people throughout the world—the place where things really happened. On June 20th, they began a European tour (France, Italy, and Spain). Four days later, John Lennon's second book, *A Spaniard in the Works*, was released. During the summer, the movie *Help!* was released, along with the Beatles' fifth studio album (also called *Help!*).

116 The Beatles having fun straightening one another's ties before a press conference held on June 12th, 1965. The day before, it was announced that they were to be appointed Members of the Most Excellent Order of the British Empire by Queen Elizabeth.

117 top and bottom The two covers of the album Help!, released in 1965. Above, the original one; below, the cover of the soundtrack of the film of the same name.

On the surface, the album was merely meant to complement the movie, which, like *A Hard Day's Night*, was a comedy, though this one was much more fantastical, centered on desparate search for Ringo, who has been kidnapped. But *Help!* was really the first album of the Beatles' new style, an album with a heavier sound that ultimately contributed to the birth of modern rock. This album belongs in the same category as Bob Dylan's "Like a Rolling Stone," The Who's "My Generation," and the Rolling Stones' "Satisfaction." The title song *Help!* demonstrated Lennon's maturity as a songwriter and sounded like a true plea for help. His "You've Got to Hide Your Love Away" is an amazing, acoustic jewel along the lines of Dylan's compositions. And McCartney's "Yesterday" is a masterpiece

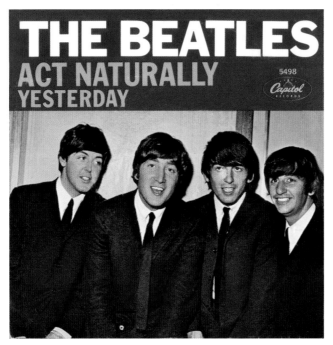

that was voted "best song of the 20th century" by a poll among critics and musicians conducted by BBC Radio 2 in 1999. The Beatles had become adults, though this was hard to see based on the absurdity of the album's accompanying film. *Help!* can thus be considered the dress rehearsal for the band's changing attitudes, while the album that demonstrated this shift most clearly is *Revolver*, released the following year (1966). The album released directly after *Help!* but before *Revolver* was titled *Rubber Soul*, which was recorded in only four weeks at the end of another American tour and released in England before Christmas.

This work was created only four months after the preceding album, and already it was like listening to another band. This was no accident. That August, the band had met Elvis in his Bel Air home, and they actually got to have a short jam session with him. Shortly after this meeting, they tried LSD for the first time, with Roger McGuinn of the Byrds and Peter Fonda. This would prove to be a fundamental experience for the Beatles, just as the discovery (again, thanks to Roger McGuinn) of Indian music would also be important. The musician Ravi Shankar and his sitar greatly influenced George Harrison. He had first seen Indian classical music being played by a group of Indian musicians during the shooting of *Help!*.

Psychedelic drugs were becoming a larger part of the cultural scene in the United States; LSD was still legal at this

118 *The cover of the single "Act Naturally," the side B of which was "Yesterday," written and sung by Paul and released in 1965 by Capitol Records.*

119 *The cover of* Rubber Soul, *which was released on December 3rd, 1965.*

point, and thousands of young people were attempting to broading their "fields of consciousness" through lisergic acid.

When the band returned to England, they had plenty to think about. In retrospect, the number of excellent songs they recorded for *Rubber Soul* is truly impressive; the album contains 14 songs in total, including "Drive My Car," "Norwegian Wood," "Nowhere Man," "Michelle," "Girl," and "In My Life." Just like *A Hard Day's Night*, all the songs on the album were original, with Lennon and McCartney responsible for nearly all of them. The song "If I Needed Someone" was written by Harrison. On "Norwegian Wood," the sitar is used for the first time on a Beatles track, played by Harrison. On "In My Life," McCartney sings about memories. The song "Nowhere Man," written mostly by Lennon, is notable for being one of the first Beatles songs not about the subject of love. On "Drive My Car," the instruments almost overshadow the lyrics of the track itself, and on "The Word," the theme of universal love is explored for the first time. The album as a whole is often viewed as an attempt by the Beatles to process everything they had seen and heard during their time in America. It's also an early example of psychedelia and progressive rock.

In August, the band performed at Shea Stadium in New York City, in front of an audience of about 56,000 persons, a new concert attendance record at the time. This was the last show of their American tour. Recording for *Rubber Soul* began in October; in the middle of this process, the four were received at Buckingham Palace to be nominated as Members of the British Empire.

After their final concert at Shea Stadium in New York, the four returned to London to receive their MBE medals.

120-121 October 26th, 1965: Policemen struggle to restrain the fans who want to enter Buckingham Palace.

121 A fan attempts to climb over the gate of Buckingham Palace.

122-123 The Beatles displaying their MBE medals, which Queen Elizabeth II awarded them at Buckingham Palace.

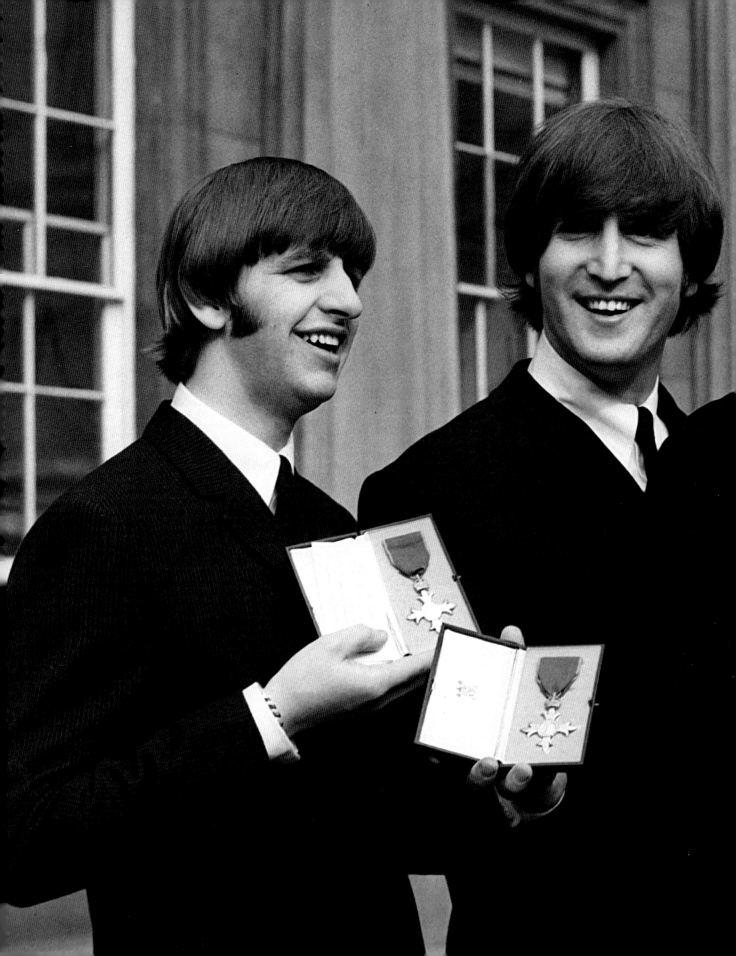

"HELP! I'm kidnapped!" "HELP! I'm lost on a tropic island!" "HELP! I'm surrounded by women!" "HELP! keep our city clean!"

STOP WORRYING!

IS ON THE WAY!

The Colorful Adventures of

THE BEATLES

are more Colorful than ever...in COLOR!

ALSO STARRING **LEO McKERN**

HELP YOURSELF TO SEVEN GREAT NEW BEATLE HITS!

ELEANOR BRON   **VICTOR SPINETTI**   **ROY KINNEAR**

PRODUCED BY **WALTER SHENSON**   SCREENPLAY BY **MARC BEHM** AND **CHARLES WOOD**   STORY BY **MARC BEHM**   DIRECTED BY **RICHARD LESTER**

EASTMANCOLOR   A WALTER SHENSON—SUBAFILMS PRODUCTION   A **UNITED ARTISTS** RELEASE

The British monarchy is also subject
TO BEATLEMANIA,
which has spread worldwide

124 *A poster of the movie Help!, directed by Richard Lester.*

125 *Lord Snowdon and Princess Margaret meet the Beatles at the premiere of the film Help!, organized by the Royal Charity and held at the London Pavilion on July 29th, 1965.*

126-127 *The playbill of the premiere of the movie Help!, which was attended by members of the royal family. The movie, directed by Richard Lester, was a great success. On the back are dedications written by the four Beatles.*

To Victor
my life's work.
tup all my sincere and
devotion and that
God rest you
truly
John (Lennon) x

a cross

Printed by
L. Delow & Co. Ltd.,
1, Southwark Bridge,
London, S.E.1

To Victor
best wishes
Ringo Starr

Dear Victor
I like you, but you
weren't as good as Mal
Paul (McCartney)

Only for you-Victor—
it would have all been possible!
George Harrison.

THE BEATLES

SEVEN NEW SONGS

HELP!!

also starring

LEO McKERN

ELEANOR BRON   VICTOR SPINETTI   ROY KINNEAR

produced by WALTER SHENSON   screenplay by MARC BEHM & CHARLES WOOD   story by MARC BEHM   directed by RICHARD LESTER

 A WALTER SHENSON SUBAFILMS Production   **EASTMAN COLOUR**   UNITED ARTISTS Production

ROYAL WORLD PREMIERE

in the gracious presence of
HER ROYAL HIGHNESS THE PRINCESS MARGARET, COUNTESS OF SNOWDON
and THE EARL OF SNOWDON

Sponsored by The Variety Club of Great Britain
to aid THE DOCKLAND SETTLEMENTS and THE VARIETY CLUB HEART FUND

on

THURSDAY 29th JULY 1965

at the

LONDON PAVILION

PICCADILLY CIRCUS

THE FILM INDUSTRY NOTICES THE BEATLES, AND *A HARD DAY'S NIGHT* IS A HUGE SUCCESS

128 The Beatles run along the River Thames in a scene from Help!, shot at the City Barge, a pub in the Strand-on-the-Green area of Chiswick, London.

128-129 Another scene from Help!: The Beatles are arrested in front of the City Barge pub in Chiswick.

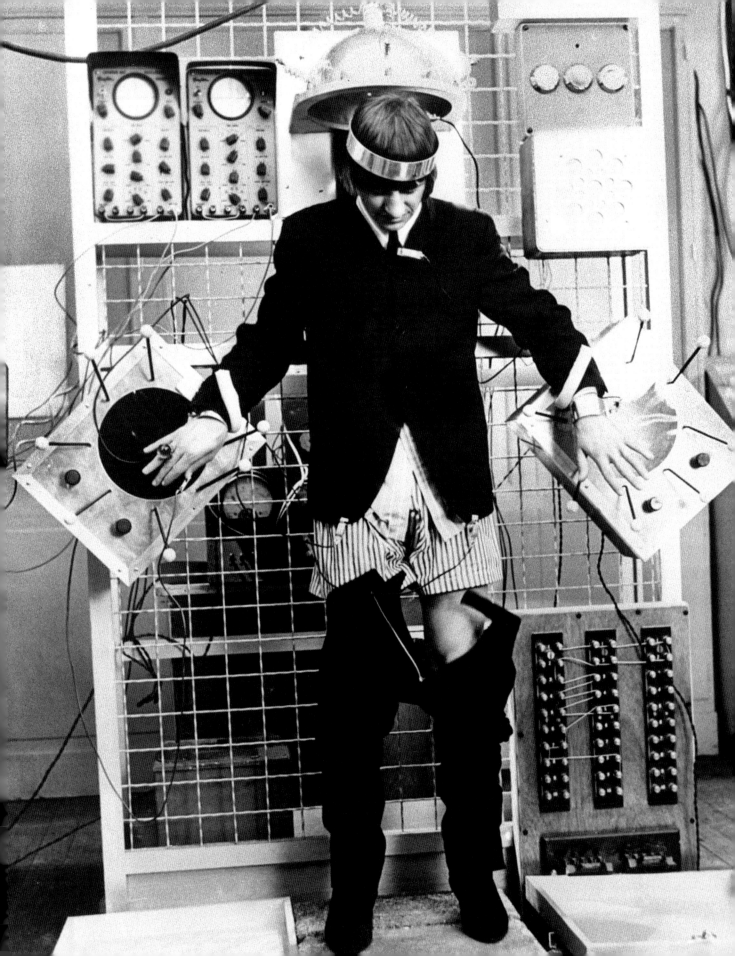

130 *Ringo Starr is strapped to a machine in* Help!.

THEY WEREN'T ACTORS, BUT THEIR INNATE CHARM TRANSLATED WELL TO THE BIG SCREEN

131 *George Harrison pushes John Lennon in a wheelchair as they attempt to pass by unnoticed in an airport (their disguises can't be called convincing).*

132 Paul McCartney and George Harrison during a
concert held in Sweden in 1965.

132-133 The Beatles during the rehearsals for the
broadcast of the ABC-TV Blackpool Night Out program,
performed at the ABC Theatre of Blackpool on August
1st, 1965.

134 *The Fab Four perform at the Palais des Expositions in Paris on June 20th, 1965.*

134-135 *The band on the terrace of the hotel they stayed in during the Paris leg of their tour in France (June 20th, 1965).*

4

1966-1969
THE GREATEST BAND
IN THE WORLD

JOHN, PAUL, GEORGE, AND RINGO;
THE BEATLES AND ROCK MUSIC,
FROM PSYCHEDELIA TO ART

January 1966 began with George Harrison and Pattie Boyd's wedding. The Beatles were continuing to grow up. Lennon was the father of Julian, and Maureen Cox had already given birth to Zak Starkey, Ringo's son. The four needed more time and space for their personal lives; they were tired of the frenetic routine of the preceding years and wanted to cultivate other interests, discover new things, and escape from the constant media attention and the roles Beatlemania had imposed on them. John Lennon's interview with Maureen Cleave, a friend of the Beatles and a journalist for the *London Evening Standard*, proved to be the last straw. In the interview, Lennon said: "Christianity will go. It will vanish and shrink. I needn't argue about that, I know I'm right and I will be proved right. We're more popular than Jesus now. I don't know which will go first—Rock 'n' Roll or Christianity. Jesus was all right, but his disciples were thick and ordinary. It's them twisting it that ruins it for me." Lennon's words didn't trigger much of a scandal in England, but in the United States, it was like a bomb had exploded. His words provoked a public outcry, fueled by the slogan: "The Beatles are bigger than Jesus." Many radio stations temporarily banned the Beatles' music and numerous preachers violently attacked them in the press, predicting that their music would help lead a generation of youngsters to perdition. There were even cases of Beatles records being burned in public bonfires. This occurred just a few months before the start of another U.S. tour, a recipe for disaster. Epstein

LENNON SAYS THE BEATLES ARE MORE POPULAR THAN JESUS, SPARKING A SCANDAL IN THE U.S.

forced Lennon to apologize and explain his statements in a press conference. "I'm not anti-God, anti-Christ, or anti-religion. I was not saying we are greater or better. From what I've read, or observed, Christianity just seems to be shrinking, to be losing contact."

The band started working on their seventh album, *Revolver*, recording it in April of 1966, just after Lennon had bought and read the book *The Psychedelic Experience* by Timothy Leary and Ralph Metzner. The album begins with one of their most revolutionary songs, "Tomorrow Never Knows," which included electro-acoustic sounds never used before in popular music. The track's lyrics were based on the *Tibetan Book of the Dead*. Other techniques used on the song include overdubbing, tape manipulation, reverse sounds, and voice filters. Simply put, this wasn't a song the band would ever be able to play in a live concert; it was a song born from studio technology, and it hinted at the end of the Beatles' careers as live performers. It also helped shift the focus away from singles, encouraging fans to see the whole album as a single piece of art.

The album was revolutionary. Its tracks included "Eleanor Rigby" by Paul, "Taxman" by George, "I'm Only Sleeping" by John, and the songs "Here There and Everywhere," "Yellow Submarine," "She Said She Said," "Good Day Sunshine," "For No One," and "Got To Get You Into My Life." Each song seemed beautiful, unique, and capable of standing on its own. All of them were created in the recording studio rather than in practice spaces, with a more intense focus on detail. The band spent 220 hours in the studio for *Revolver*, compared to the 80 hours they had spent recording *Rubber Soul*.

1 9 6 6

140 Adolescents in the United States protest against the Beatles by throwing the band's albums, fanzines, books, and gadgets into a bonfire.

141 Another photo of youngsters at a 'Beatles Burning' organized by the radio station WAYX-AM Georgia. The protests erupted after Lennon stated that the band had become more popular that Jesus.

RADIO STATIONS BOYCOTT THE BEATLES, PROTESTS ARE ORGANIZED, AND THE BAND'S ALBUMS ARE BURNED. LENNON APOLOGIZES

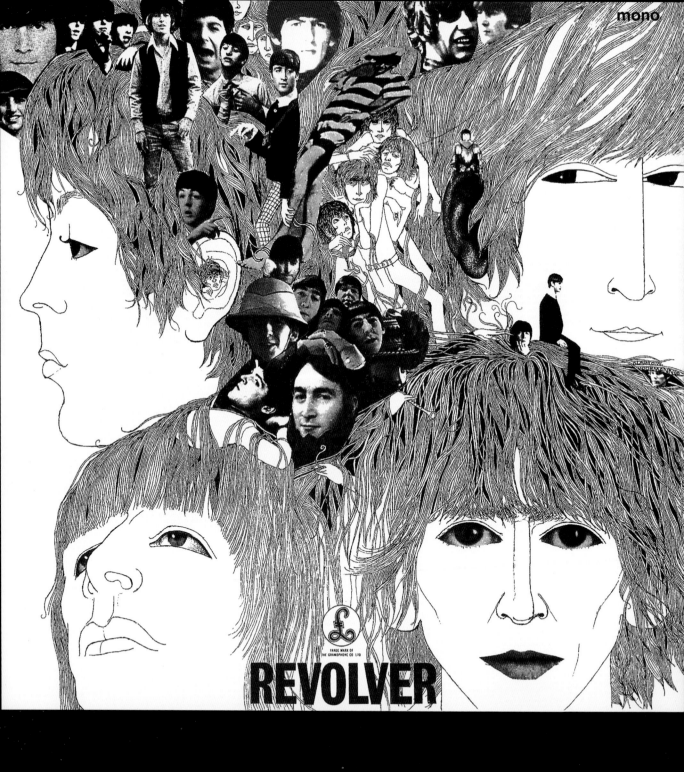

REVOLVER

142 The cover of Revolver, designed by Klaus Voorman, a friend of the Beatles from the Hamburg days.

143 The Fab Four in 1966, after having dinner in the dining car of a train.

By the end of June, the recordings were completed, and the band went on tour again, this time to Germany. In early July, they went to Tokyo, where they gave five concerts at the Budokan Arena. According to newspapers, 3,000 policemen were stationed throughout the city to prevent public incidents. Officers were also placed in every row at the Budokan. The Beatles were unfortunately confined to their hotel, going out only for their concerts. This was partly because the police claimed that death threats had

A diplomatic incident occurred in Manila when the band didn't show up after being invited to the presidential palace by Imelda Marcos.

been made against the band. The situation and atmosphere in Japan depressed the group's members, and things didn't imrpove when they traveled to Manila. The Philippines was ruled by the dictator Ferdinand Marcos. When the Beatles arrived in the capitol, the more than 5,000 screaming fans were surrounded by shocking numbers of armed policemen and soldiers. The fear and tension in the air was palpable, and the band found it difficult to process. Marcos' wife Imelda invited the Beatles to the presidential residence so they could meet their three children, who were great fans of the band. The invitation was extended in an informal manner, and Epstein decided to refuse it, despite pressure from the British Embassy. The band thus found itself in a complex situation, to say the least. TV coverage assumed the band would appear at the Marcos' residence, but the guests of honor failed to show up.

144-145 Another photograph of the Beatles in 1966 while going from one city to another during their European tour.

146 The Beatles onstage during a concert in Germany, on one of their last tours (June 1st, 1966).

146-147 The audience surrounds the stage of the band's concert at the Circus Krone in Munich.

3,000 POLICEMEN GUARD THE BUDOKAN IN TOKYO AFTER THE BAND SUPPOSEDLY RECEIVES DEATH THREATS

148 Policemen control the state entrance at the Nippon Budokan in Tokyo during the Beatles' concert on June 30th, 1966.

149 The band goes on stage at the Nippon Budokan, Tokyo.

The reaction by Marcos and his wife was severe. They called off all protection for the Beatles, who, after only two concerts, decided to leave the Philippines as quickly as possible. Their departure sparked protests, threats, gunshots, and physical aggression against Epstein and Mal Evans (an assistant to the Beatles). Many Filipinos were offended by the band's behavior. On their way back to England, they stopped in India, where George was able to buy a sitar.

In August, after the release of *Revolver*, the band again hit the road, this time in the United States for another series of concerts that would last a month. But by this time, the Beatles had had enough of concerts and appearances. Beatlemania had consumed them; they felt burnt out, and the audiences in the stadiums and theaters screamed so much during their sets that the band could hardly hear their own instruments. They were also sick of the daily routines imposed by extended tours, which had become a straitjacket of live performances, press conferences, and hotel stays that could feel soulless, especially for John. Unsurprisingly, they decided to stop giving live concerts; their last one was held in San Francisco on August 29th, 1966, at Candlestick Park.

The 'Fabulous Four' were tired of the lives they had led during the last three or four years. Each member now had different interests. They were still united, but their personalities had matured in separate directions. George and Pattie decided to return to India to stay for an extended period, as George wanted to learn to play the sitar from one of India's great musicians, Ravi Shankar. John began an acting career and went to Spain to play a role in *How I Won the War*, directed by Richard Lester. Paul became increasingly interested in classical music and composing, and he set to work on his first solo composition, the soundtrack of the movie *The Family Way*, directed by Roy Boulting. And Ringo concentrated on his family life, later joining John in Spain.

150 George Harrison and Paul McCartney (right) try out a sitar in the Rikhi Ram musical instruments store in New Delhi, India (July 6th, 1966).

151 John Lennon and Ringo Starr converse during a break in the shooting of the film How I Won The War, *directed by Richard Lester, in which Lennon played one of the protagonists. It was shot in Spain in autumn 1966.*

November 1966 was certainly a pivotal month in the history of the Beatles. On November 7th, John Lennon met Yoko Ono at the Indica Gallery in London. The Japanese artist had an exhibition there titled *Unfinished Paintings*. Lennon was curious and was struck by Yoko's art and her personality. On November 18th, while on an airplane returning to England from Nairobi, Kenya, where he had stayed with Jane Asher and Mal Evans, Paul began formulating the project that would later become the album *Sgt. Pepper's Lonely Hearts Club Band*. Paul describes this process in Barry Miles's book, *Many Years from Now*: "We were fed up with being Beatles. We really hated that fucking four little mop-top boys approach. We were not boys, we were men. It was all gone, all that boy shit, all that screaming, we didn't want it any more. Plus, we'd got turned on to pot and thought of ourselves as artists rather than just performers. There was now more to it; not only had John and I

1967: the beginning of a revolution IN YOUTH CULTURE as young people throughout the world try to change the rules of the game and society by introducing new, utopian concepts

been writing, George had been writing, we'd been in films, John had written books, so it was natural that we should become artists. Then suddenly on the plane I got this idea. I thought, Let's not be ourselves. Let's develop altar egos so we're not having to project an image which we know. It would be much more free . . . So it wouldn't be John or Paul singing, it would be the members of this band . . . I thought, we can run this philosophy through the whole album; with this alter ego band, it won't be us making all that sound, it won't be the Beatles, it'll be this other band, so we'll be able to lose our identities in this."

Everything was changing once again. This was clearest in the recording studio, where the band was determined to make one of their most creative and experimental albums to date. On November 24th, they recorded the first take of a new song by John called *Strawberry Fields Forever*. This song was a moment of rebirth for the band. New sounds, a new atmosphere of creativity, new lyrics, and a spanking new image. They discarded their previous maxim to always dress in unison. Each member began dressing as he pleased, and they also abandoned the signature mop-top, letting their hair grow long. The year 1967 was on its way, energized by the revolutionary spirit of youth culture. Everywhere in the world, young people were changing the rules of the game and rejecting the society established by their parents. They hoped to recreate reality through simple but fundamental concepts like equality, joy, and universal love. This marked the birth of hippie culture, which emphatically repudiated consumer society and made San Francisco its mecca. At the same time, many universities (especially University of California, Berkeley) became organizational hubs of this new culture. Most world leaders were considered enemies; direct democracy was championed, and violence (in all its many forms) was frowned upon. London soon began to reflect this culture of creativity—the city sparkled with psychedelic colors; the shops on Carnaby Street sold vibrant clothing that slowly began to invade the outlets and boutiques in wealthier neighborhoods. Fasion became a must for anyone hoping to keep pace with the times. Youth culture seemed to be following the slogans of Jerry Rubin, the American social activist and anti-war leader: "Don't trust anyone over thirty." Long hair became the ID-card for like-minded youngsters who fought for the same values.

"We want the world and we want it now!" shouted Jim Morrison of The Doors, and hundreds of thousands of young people from New York to Berlin, from London to Tokyo, shouted with him, all happening within an explosion of desire and creativity that remains unparalleled to this day. The year 1967 marked the rise of Jimi Hendrix, who had dazzled the elite guitarists of London (including John Lennon, Eric Clapton, Jeff Beck, and Pete Townshend) with his energy and solos.

154 Two photographs taken during the shooting of the Strawberry Fields Forever *film clip, shot in late January 1967 at*

1967

This year also witnessed the birth of Human Be-In, an event held at Golden Gate Park in San Francisco. Personalities like Allen Ginsberg, Jerry Rubin, and Abbie Hoffman appeared alongside bands like the Grateful Dead. The event became the model for concerts throughout the late 60s and early 70s. Another important rock festival was held in Monterey, California (the Monterey International Pop Music Festival). It featured The Who, whose members smashed their instruments onstage, and Jimi Hendrix, who famously set his guitar on fire. Rock music became synonymous with youth, and this new sound encompassed a potent mix of reality and dreams which couldn't be fully captured by TV, radio, or newspapers. These outlets were both enamored and horrified by the rapid growth of this new culture. Hippie culture began spreading to youngsters who weren't necessarily interested in protests or political activism. In short, the culture had begun seeping into the suburbs, and many people were attracted simply because of the vibrant clothes and music.

For the Beatles, considered a symbol of free love for all young people, 1967 was another year of big changes, starting with the recording of "Penny Lane," "When I'm 64," and "A Day in the Life" at Abbey Road. Paul was right in observing that they were no longer the Beatles; there were enormous differences between these later songs and earlier songs like "She Loves You," released only three years before. The rest of the band liked Paul's conceptual approach, and they got to work recording the new album in February. During this time, they released what many consider to be the best single in the history of rock, the double A-side single featuring "Strawberry Fields Forever" and "Penny Lane."

San Francisco hosts the Human Be-In, and the first major rock festival is held in Monterey. The Beatles have also changed radically.

Between February and April, they recorded the album that best demonstrates their maturity as songwriters (and a true masterpiece of the psychedelic era): *Sgt. Pepper's Lonely Hearts Club Band*. There are certain albums that come to define popular culture. *Sgt. Pepper's* serves that purpose for the 20th century. It ushered in a new era in fashion and creativity, and indeed the album is often the one people think of when they remember the Beatles.

Released on June 1st, 1967, the album changed the course of history. It signaled the closing of the1960s and developed a cult following that has endured to this day. Are we exaggerating? Nope, the album is that good. Its songs include: "With a Little Help From My Friends," sung by Ringo Starr; "Lucy in the Sky with Diamonds," mistakenly considered a homage to LSD (the acronym of the title); "She's Leaving Home," "Getting Better," and the impressive concluding song, "A Day in the Life."

STG. PEPPER'S LONELY HEARTS CLUB BAND,
THE MASTERPIECE
of the psychedelic era

These were songs destined to remain steady favorites through the decades. They penetrated the collective imagination and consciousness of youth culture, so much that we can't help still feeling captivated by the album's rich sound and complex, studio-produced patterns that twist and turn themselves into simple melodies. An essential work of British psychedelia, the album incorporates a range of stylistic influences, including vaudeville, circus, music hall, avant-garde, and Western and Indian classical music. Echoes of India can be heard on the song "Within You Without You." Vaudeville sounds appear on "When I'm 64."

156 The legendary and innovative cover of Stg. Pepper's Lonely Hearts Club Band *(1967), the album that greatly influenced the culture of the 1960s.*

Then there's the album's famous cover. The Beatles are surrounded by historical figures from different fields, a stroke of genius on the part of one of the leading English pop artists at the time, Peter Blake, who essentially chose the colors of what would later become known as the Summer of Love. Thus, we can't consider *Sgt. Pepper's* as merely an album or a collection of songs. It was a once-in-a-lifetime work, a jewel that has managed to escape the ravages of time. It was created by the band when they were at their artistic peak. Knowing they would never have to perform these songs live, the band adopted an experimental approach to composition and recording that treated the studio as an instrument itself. Many also consider *Sgt. Pepper's* the first concept album for its dedication to the fictional Sgt. Pepper band.

Soon the Summer of Love would begin in San Francisco, with the hippies ready to color the world with flower power.

158 and 159 The Fab Four joke for photographers during a media appearance for Stg. Pepper. *The album was influenced by the Beach Boys and displayed a new refinement in rock music.*

Shortly after the release of *Sgt. Pepper's*, the Beatles began recording another masterpiece. This time, it was a new single that marvelously epitomized flower power, pacifism, and the desire to change the world: "All You Need Is Love." There seemed to be no end to their creativite energies. By this time, their fame allowed them total freedom in the studio. Abbey Road was at their disposal 24 hours a day, and the band found itself with plenty of time to create, as they were no longer burdened by live performances, press conferences, and TV specials. The planned to use this time to produce a constant stream of new music. There was also plenty of time for new experiences: Lennon became increasingly involved with Yoko Ono. McCartney met Linda Eastman in May and fell in love with her. He also caused a media scandal in an interview by admitting he had taken LSD. Additionally, the four signed a petition to legalize marijuana, which was published in *The Times* on July 24th, right in the middle of the Summer of Love. In July and August 1967, they traveled together to Greece on vacation, where they considered buying a small island. Then George and Patti made another trip to India and stopped in San Francisco on their way back home.

In late August, the Beatles met Maharishi Mahesh Yogi at a conference in London that Pattie Boyd had taken them to. They were impressed by the guru's words and spiritual teachings and decided to follow him to Bangor, Wales to participate in a ten-day seminar on transcendental meditation. Mick Jagger and Marianne Faithfull were in attendance as well. But the band didn't stay the full ten days. On August 27th, they learned that Brian Epstein had died of an overdose in his Chapel Street home in London. This was a terrible blow to the band. Epstein wasn't merely their manager; he was a close friend who had been there since the beginning—the person who organized their activities, handled their finances, and helped them realize their many creative projects. The band thought of him as an older brother.

160 The Beatles with the placards used during a worldwide broadcast of "All You Need Is Love" in 1967, a perfect example of the pacifism that was beginning to permeate the songs written by John Lennon.

161 The band in the studio rehearsing "All You Need Is Love."

162 The Beatles meet Maharishi Mahesh Yogi on September 4th, 1967. From left: McCartney, Jane Asher, Patti Harrison, Mike McCartney, Starr, Maureen Starr, Lennon, Harrison, and the Maharishi.

162-163 The band with the Maharishi on a train on the way to Bangor, in northern Wales, on August 29th, 1967.

The *Magical Mystery Tour* was inspired by the bus trip Ken Kesey and his Merry Pranksters made from one end of the U.S. to the other.

On Septemebr 1st, after Epstein had been buried, the group met at Paul's home in St. John's Woods, London. They discussed the idea of a trip to India to see the Maharishi. They also discussed a movie proposal that they had been considering for a long time: *Magical Mystery Tour*. Paul was inspired by what Ken Kesey and his Merry Pranksters were doing in America. The Pranksters toured California on a school bus painted in flower power colors, a kind of surreal art experiment in line with the psychedelic times. Another motivation for the movie was to satisfy their fans, who couldn't see them perform live since their decision to stop touring.

Paul convinced the others that, after the successes of *A Hard Day's Night* and *Help!*, it was time for the Beatles to direct their own movie.

Shooting began the following week and continued through early November. It was frequently interrupted by recording sessions for the songs on the movie's soundtrack and by meetings to determine how the band would be managed going forward. The movie *How I Won the War* also premiered during this time (on October 18th, 1967), which John Lennon starred in, and the group released a new single, "Hello, Goodbye," which soon topped the charts in both England the U.S.

164 *September 15th, 1967: The Beatles and a group of walk-ons prepare to embark on a journey aboard the* Magical Mystery Tour *bus.*

165 *The band on the* Magical Mystery Tour *bus in one of the scenes from the film.*

166 *The Beatles in multicolored clothing perform "Your Mother Should Know" for the grand finale of* Magical Mystery Tour *at the West Malling Air Station in Kent on September 24th, 1967.*

167 *A poster advertising the film* Magical Mystery Tour *in the United Kingdom. The film was not well received. As a result, the United States premiere scheduled for Easter weekend in 1967 was canceled.*

The Beatles are back in the legendary film made by and starring The Beatles.

The Beatles singing "The Fool on the Hill", "I Am The Walrus", "Strawberry Fields Forever", "All You Need is Love" and more.

Let yourself go—The Beatles will come and take you away in **Magical Mystery Tour.**

The band had many other projects in the works. Ringo made his acting debut in the movie *Candy*, shot in Italy. It was directed by Christian Marquand and featured an all-star cast that included Ewa Aulin, Charles Aznavour, Marlon Brando, Richard Burton, James Coburn, John Huston, and Walter Matthau. Meanwhile, Paul and John were thinking about opening a shop in the heart of London called the Apple Boutique. It was conceived as something between a shop and a museum. In McCartney's words, it was meant to be: "a beautiful place where beautiful people can find beautiful things." The boutique opened on December 7th, 1967, on the corner of Baker Street and Paddington Street in Marylebone, London. It remained in business for only eight months, as it was plagued by shoplifting on the part of both potential clients and the shop personnel themselves. In the end, the boutique resulted in a loss of roughly £200,000.

Unfortunately, *Magical Mystery Tour* didn't fare much better. It was broadcasted on the BBC in black and white on December 26th, 1967, and was received poorly by critics and audiences alike. Although the movie appeared to be a setback, the album, released a few weeks earlier, was a critical and commercial hit despite generally being considered a lesser

The Beatles opened the Apple Boutique on December 7th, 1967, on the corner of Baker Street and Paddington Street in Marylebone, London.

work compared to their earlier albums. The album feels like a second chapter to the psychedelic adventures of *Sgt. Pepper's*. In fact, *Magical Mystery Tour* consists only partly of the movie soundtrack, as it included a few songs that didn't make it onto *Sgt. Pepper's Lonely Hearts Club Band*. Originally released as a double EP that contained the songs of the movie, it was eventually turned into a bona fide album and released in the U.S. on November 27th, 1967. Surprisingly, despite a flurry of negative reviews, it became one of the most successful Beatles records. In its first three weeks, it sold more than any other record in history, netting Capitol Records millions of dollars. The six songs from the soundtrack rank among the best the Beatles ever created, beginning with the title song, which was composed primarily by McCartney in a style similar to the one used on *Sgt. Pepper's*. Once again, the album felt like something no other pop group could create. It's composition is a mixture of memories and magical excursions into the future. Unique flourishes appearing on the album include winds and keyboards,

distortion, and many other special effects that became staples of modern recording. There are masterpieces such as "The Fool on the Hill" by McCartney and Harrison's beautiful "Blue Jay Way," along with the only instrumental piece in the Beatles' entire canon of recordings: "Flying" (it was also the only song credited to all four Beatles). The nostalgic "Your Mother Should Know" was written by McCartney. Perhaps the most outstanding song on the album, or at least the most interesting, is Lennon's "I am the Walrus," an unsurpassable psychedelic gem that merges complexity with irony. Many of the other songs released on the album were previously recorded singles such as "Baby You're a Rich Man."

These songs came from the *Sgt. Pepper's* era. The marvelous "Penny Lane" and "Strawberry Fields Forever" help round out the album. Despite its initial criticism, it's a magnificent album—the last one recorded before tensions among the four members began to tug at the fabric of the band.

168 December 7th, 1967: A crowd gathers in front of the Apple Boutique, at the corner of Baker Street and Paddington Street in London.

169 The cover of the album Magical Mystery Tour.

1968

The second Beatle to begin working on solo music projects (after Paul, who wrote the soundtrack for the movie *The Family Way*) was George. He left for India in early 1968 to record the soundtrack for the movie *Onyricon*. He also wanted to record music with a group of Indian musicians in Mumbai. When he returned to England, the four began working together again. In early February of 1968, they recorded "Lady Madonna" and "Across the Universe." The former was written by Paul, and John wrote the latter. Then, in the middle of the month, the band decided to follow George to Rishikesh to explore transcendental meditation. The trip was meant as a religious retreat, as the band would study meditation with Marahishi Mahesh Yogi. Their group included the singer Donovan Philips Leitch, Mia Farrow and her sister, Mike Love of the Beach Boys, and many others. For the Beatles, the trip served as a gateway to Indian culture and music. And due to the media that followed the band, many young people in the United Kingdom and the U.S. were exposed to the same things. This chapter in the band's history would prove to be the last in which they were committed to writing music together.

The trip to Rishikesh led an entire generation to India by revealing its spirituality, its culture and its search for wisdom.

The Beatles returned separately from India; Ringo stayed for two weeks, Paul a little more than a month, and John and George for almost two months. Each was searching for his own path and, while each member was still officially a Beatle, it seemed that the magic had been lost. This was especially true for George, who suffered from the domination of the Lennon/McCartney composer duo. During this time, John, who had fallen in love with Yoko and had separated from Cynthia, discovered new forms of artistic expression and became increasingly attached to his new partner. Paul had broken free from the need to include John in all his music writing; for months now, he had led a completely independent life and had contemplated a solo career. Ringo was arguably the only member with a strong interest in preserving the band, and in many books about the Beatles, Ringo is often acknowleged as the glue that kept the four from drifting apart completely.

170-171 The Beatles and their friends in Rishikesh, India in March 1968. The group includes Ringo with his wife Maureen, Jane Asher, Paul, George and his wife Patti, John and Cynthia Lennon, Mal Evans, Mia Farrow and her sister Prudence, Donovan and his girlfriend Jenny Boyd, and the Beach Boy Mike Love.

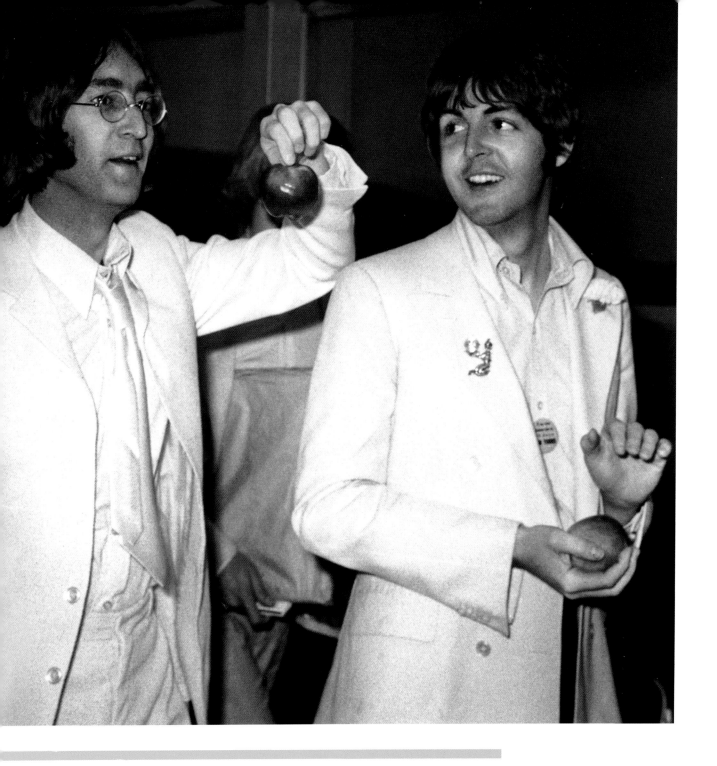

172 Lennon and McCartney at an airport in London upon their return from a trip to the United States to promote the newly established Apple Corps. They are dressed in white and, naturally, are holding apples.

173 The interior of Apple Tailoring, the apparel shop owned by the Beatles that opened in 1968 at 161 King's Road, London. It was managed by the designer John Crittle.

THE BAND CREATED APPLE CORPS AND DIVIDED IT INTO FIVE DIVISIONS: APPLE RECORDS, APPLE ELECTRONICS, APPLE FILMS, APPLE PUBLISHING, AND APPLE RETAIL

When they returned from India and before they went to the studio to record more songs, the band became occupied with the establishment of their multimedia corporation: Apple Corps. The corporation consisted of five divisions: Apple Records, Apple Electronics, Apple Films, Apple Publishing, and Apple Retail (the last division was in charge not only of the Boutique but also of a second shop, Apple Tailoring, on King's Road, which had opened on May 22nd, 1968).

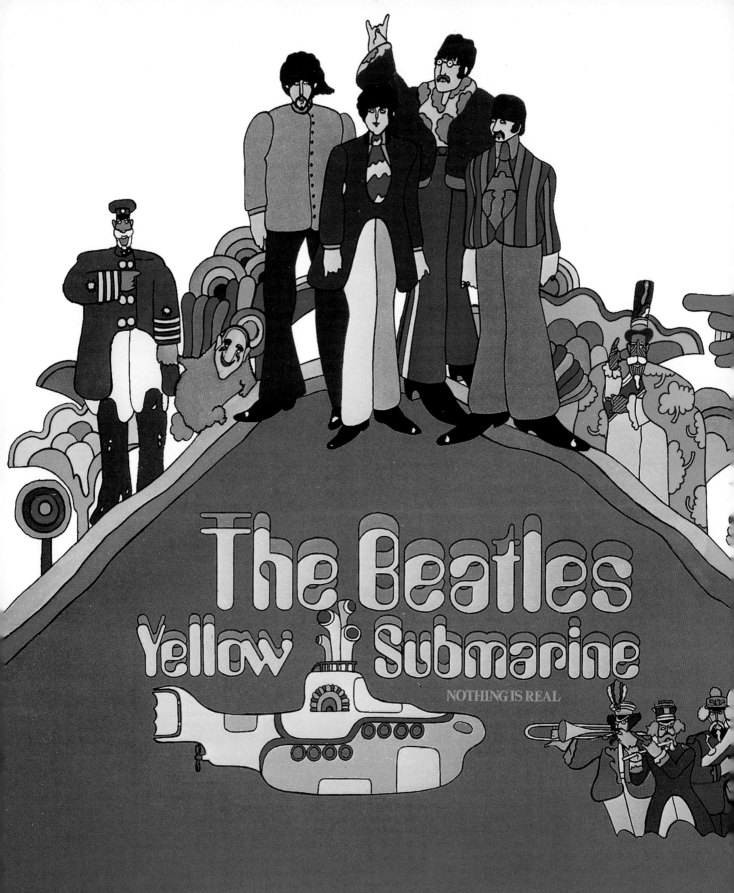

In June of 1968, a new movie was released, this one an animated cartoon: *Yellow Submarine*. The Beatles' collaboration on the project was very limited, but the movie, the band's last psychedelic creation, contains a few original songs, including Harrison's irresistible "It's All Too Much."

174-175 *The famous cover of* Yellow Submarine *(1968)*.

175 *Four badges, each featuring a Beatles character from Yellow Submarine. Clockwise: Paul McCartney, John Lennon, Ringo Starr, and George Harrison.*

IN JUNE OF 1968, THE BEATLES RELEASE THE
ANIMATED CARTOON *YELLOW SUBMARINE,*
THEIR LAST PSYCHEDELIC CREATION

176 John Lennon's animated character in a scene in Yellow Submarine, released in 1968
and written by Erich Segal and Lee Minoff, among others.

177 An animated John Lennon and George Harrison in a scene from Yellow Submarine.
The art director was Heinz Edelmann, and the film was directed by George Dunning.

178 John Lennon and Yoko Ono in a recording studio in 1968, probably listening to the recordings of their album
Unfinished Music No. 1: Two Virgins.

179 The cover of the single "Back in the U.S.S.R."

Naturally, business wasn't the group's main interest in releasing more music. The band's time in India just happened to be one of their most productive periods, and they had written a huge number of original songs (meaning mostly John, Paul, and George). In an attempt to preserve the band, and also to show themselves how much they had developed as artists in recent months, they decided to record a double album. They got together on May 24th in George's Kinfauns house in Surrey, where they recorded acoustic demos of a whopping 27 songs, 19 of which eventually comprised their new album, titled *The Beatles*. The album cover was completely white and featured no true title, only the name of the band in white over a white background, making the group's name virtually illegible. On the inside of the album, for the first time, no photographs of the complete band were included. Instead, four separate portraits are displayed, as if to underscore the deep differences in approach and personality which had begun to impact the survival of the band. These diverging personalities resulted in conflict during the album's recording sessions, in part because of Yoko Ono's presence. Despite all the drama, the album is a crowning achievement of experimentation and ingenuity, and many musical styles and genres are represented: avant-garde, pop, acoustic, electronic, ska, folk, noise, and the residue of psychedelic music. "We had left Sgt. Pepper's band to play in his sunny Elysian Fields and were now striding out in new directions without a map," Paul McCartney explained. Some songs on the album are sweet, reflecting back to the band's earlier work (Paul's "Blackbird," for example). Others are obviously post-psychedelic, like John's "Dear Prudence." George's song "While My Guitar Gently Weeps" is a classic, and it features a guitar solo by Eric Clapton, who made a guest appearance. "Revolution" is an avant-garde song inspired by the political protests of early 1968. "Helter Skelter" is essentially hard rock, and many critics consider it an early example of heavy metal.

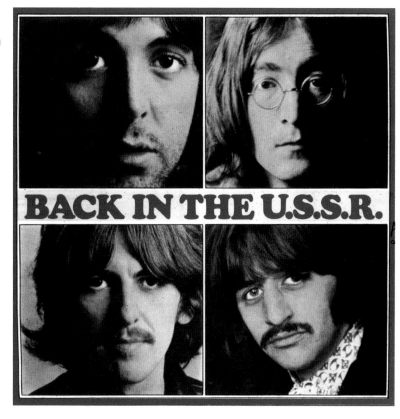

Now back from India, the band records *The Beatles*, also known as "The White Album," a double album that showcases their diverging personalities and musical interests.

180 A copy of the single "Hey Jude," released in 1968. Note the Apple Records logo in the middle of the disc.

181 The manuscript of the lyrics of "Hey Jude," the best-selling single of all time, written by Paul McCartney. This item was sold at an auction in 2002 for more than 130,000 euro.

Hey Jude don't make it bad,
take a sad song and make it better,
Remember to let her into your heart,
then you can start to make it better.

Hey Jude don't be afraid
You were made to go out and get her,
the minute you let her under your skin
Then you'll begin to make it better.

And anytime you feel the pain
hey Jude refrain don't carry the world upon
your shoulders

For well you know that's it, a fool who plays it cool
by making his (life world) a little colder.

Hey Jude don't let me down.
She had found you now make it better
Remember to let her into your heart,
then you can start to make it better.

So let it out and let it in, hey Jude begin
you waiting for someone to perform with
+ don't you know that it's just you

Thanks to the tension in the group, Ringo decided to leave the band on August 22nd. As he stated at the time, he wasn't playing well and felt "unloved" by the other three. He left the studio during a session and went off for two weeks. But the Beatles without Ringo simply wasn't the Beatles, so John, Paul, and George begged their friend to return. Nobody except those in the band's most intimate entourage knew what was happening. In fact, on August 30th, they had even released a new single, the earth-shatteringly lovely "Hey Jude." Ringo returned on September 3rd, and the following day, the four were at Twickenham Studios to record "Hey Jude" and "Revolution" for television.

During the summer, they were all extremely busy. George worked with Ravi Shankar and produced Jackie Lomax's recordings for the newborn Apple label, and Paul was doing the same with various artists like Mary Hopkin. In the meantime, Paul had separated from Jane Asher. John embarked on his pacifist projects with Yoko Ono by planting acorns for peace at Coventry Cathedral, and they inaugurated their first exhibition, *You Are Here*, in London. John's wife Cynthia asked for a divorce around this time. The recordings for the new album ended on October 14th, 1968, just before the police arrested John and Yoko (who was pregnant) for drug possession (this happened on October 18th).

The arrest was at Ringo's apartment in Montagu Square, London.

John and Yoko begin a series of pacifist art projects, but on October 18th, 1968, they are arrested in London for drug possession.

182 *Yoko Ono and John Lennon at the 1968 Christmas party held in the Apple Corps offices in Savile Row, London.*

183 *John and Yoko, surrounded by policemen, leave the courtroom of the Marylebone Magistrates' Court, where they were charged with drug possession.*

The private lives of John and Yoko began to dominate the news cycle. Yoko was the center of John's life, and when she had a miscarriage, he was shattered. Paul went to New York with Linda Eastman, his new girlfriend. George was totally absorbed in his solo music. All this activity resulted in many solo projects: November 1st saw the release of *Wonderwall Music* by George Harrison, and on November 30th, Lennon and Ono's extremely experimental album *Two Virgins* came out. Between these dates, what became known as "The White Album" was released, topping the charts in England and the U.S.

184 *Paul McCartney playing the trumpet in front of his dog Martha at a public gathering on December 12th, 1968.*

185 *Linda Eastman talks with Paul McCartney during a press conference in 1967 for Stg. Pepper's Lonely Hearts Club Band. They married in 1969.*

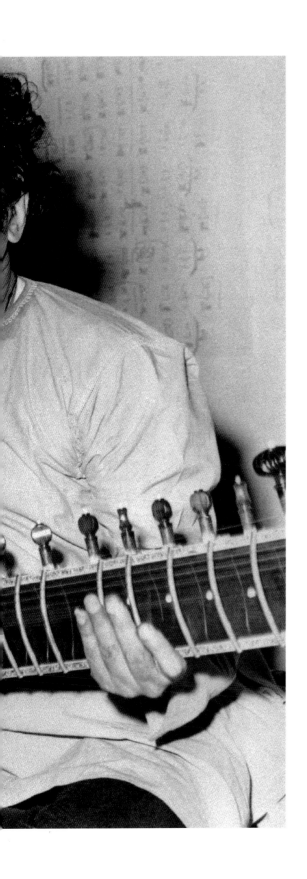

GEORGE HARRISON DEVELOPS A STRONG INTEREST IN INDIAN MUSIC AND TAKES SITAR LESSONS FROM THE GREAT RAVI SHANKAR

More solo projects followed; on December 1st, Harrison released another album, *Electronic Sound*, which was just as experimental as Lennon and Ono's recent album.

On December 11th, John played with another band for the first time (The Dirty Mac). The Dirty Mac were a one-time supergroup consisting of John Lennon, Eric Clapton, Keith Richards, and Mitch Mitchell. Lennon organized the group for the Rolling Stones' TV special, titled *The Rolling Stones Rock and Roll Circus*.

186-187 *George Harrison and Indian musician Ravi Shankar during a vacation in Southern California in 1968.*

Each member began to drift his own way. This development didn't suit McCartney. He decided to meet with the other three to propose a new project. He suggested a return to their musical roots: only the four of them with their instruments and minus all the recording studio technology. They would rehearse for a big end-of-show concert at Twickenham Studios. These rehearsals would be filmed so that the audience could see the process of writing and recording rock songs. The others agreed, although they weren't convinced that they should go back to playing live. They did appreciate the idea of returning to their roots, especially George, who had just performed in an acoustic set in America with Bob Dylan and the Band. The recording sessions of this new project, provisionally titled *Get Back*, began on January 2nd, 1969, in Twickenham Studios, but it quickly

The Beatles during their last
C O N C E R T
on the roof of Apple Corps in London

devolved into a kind of psychodrama filmed under the direction of Michael Lindsay-Hogg. Paul tried to control the recordings of the band, but this only triggered a negative reaction from the others, especially Harrison, who found it difficult to tolerate McCartney's constant 'suggestions.' Furthermore, it seemed that Lennon was mentally absent; he arrived late to many sessions and was frequently under the influence of various drugs. It wasn't uncommon for Lennon to be oblivious of the decisions made by the rest of the band. He stayed by Yoko's side and objected to the presence of so many cameras.

188-189 January 30th, 1969: The Beatles perform live for the last time on the roof of Apple Corps in London. The set was organized and filmed for the documentary Let It Be, *directed by Michael Lindsay-Hogg.*

To make matters worse, the studio was cold, the working hours trying, and, although the band rehearsed and recorded plenty of new material, the atmosphere among the four was toxic. For George, the situation had become intolerable, and on January 10th, 1969, he chose to quit the band, stating that he would be willing to return only if they abandoned the concert project and stopped rehearsing at Twickenham. The other three met at Ringo's house the next day and eventually decided that George was right. Harrison returned on January 15th, and on January 21st, the band resumed recording, this time in the basement of the new Apple headquarters at 3 Savile Row, London. Harrison also had a card up his sleeve: he brought a new keyboard player with him to the studio to defuse the tension. The keyboard player was Billy Preston. He added a fresh sound and perspective to the recordings and, above all, helped keep the band on its best behavior. The four, plus Preston, actually went so far as to give a live concert, essentially for no one, on the roof of the Apple Building in London on January 30th, 1969. It was a brief live set that the police interrupted because they considered it an illegal public disturbance. The so-called Rooftop Concert was the Beatles' last public performance, though the audience consisted only of a few dozen

John Lennon and Yoko Ono marry at Gibraltar. Paul McCartney and Linda Eastman marry in London.

persons scattered here and there on the rooftops around the building and on the sidewalk of Savile Row. Sadly, the *Get Back* project didn't get off the ground and was officially shelved. The band met again on February 3rd in the Apple offices to further discuss who should manage the affairs of the group in place of the late Brian Epstein. Tensions exploded. Harrison, Lennon, and Ringo were in favor of having businessman Allen Klein manage the band, while McCartney wanted to put everything into the hands of the law office belonging to Linda Eastman's family (Linda later became McCartney's wife).

This marked the beginning of the end, as the two sides couldn't reach an agreement. In March, McCartney married Linda, and Lennon married Yoko, and the band went its separate ways.

190 *Yoko Ono and John Lennon pose for photographers while exhibiting their wedding certificate (March 24th, 1969). They married on March 20th in the registrar's office of the British Consulate. Behind them is the Rock of Gibraltar.*

191 *Paul McCartney and Linda Eastman after leaving the Marylebone Registry Office, where they have just married (March 12th, 1969). With them is Heather, Linda's daughter from a previous marriage, and the dog Martha.*

However, by April of 1969, the Beatles had returned to the recording studio at Paul's insistence to make their eleventh studio album, *Abbey Road*. The album was nothing short of a miracle. The band was aware that this might be the last time they would ever cut a record together, and they all did their very best to finish the recordings. To this day, when one listens to the tracks of *Abbey Road* (like "Come Together," "Oh! Darling," "Something," and "Here Comes the Sun"), the feelings produced are a complex knot of sadness, joy, and hope. The lovely final medley (not including the hidden "Her Majesty" track) on side two of the record is titled "The End" and clearly signifies the conclusion of the Beatles' musical adventure: "And in the end, the love you take / is equal to the love you make." One gets the impression that the four were in a true state of grace. The creativity, emotional expression, and communicative ability of the band proved perfectly intact despite the tension.

THE ZEBRA CROSSING
IN FRONT OF EMI'S ABBEY ROAD STUDIOS
in London has become a national monument

The album was released on September 26th, 1969, and took the fourth spot of the best-selling albums of the 1960s. The album's cover also became famous. The four members of the band are featured walking through the crosswalk of Abbey Road in London. This crosswalk has become a national monument and is visited every year by thousands of tourists from all over the world. Despite early criticism that the Beatles had lost their touch, many now consider the album one of their best.

On September 12th, after being invited to play at the Toronto Peace Festival and having

192 The iconic cover of the album Abbey Road, *recorded in 1969. It consisted of the band's last official recordings. From left to right: Harrison, McCartney, Starr, and Lennon walk on the zebra crossing in front of EMI's Abbey Road Studios.*

agreed to perform with the Plastic Ono Band, John decided to leave the Beatles. He informed Allen Klein of his decision, and on September 20th, when the band met to sign a new contract that Klein had arranged with EMI, he finally told the others. Since they had committed themselves to the release of two albums, they asked John not tell anyone about this decision. In any case, the band was over, and the year 1969 ended with John performing with the Plastic Ono Band, George going on tour with Delaney and Bonnie, Paul playing with the band Badfinger, and Ringo acting with Peter Sellers in the film *The Magic Christian* and recording a solo album. John and Yoko also released their *Wedding Album*, and John returned

194 An amusing photograph of Peter Sellers and Ringo Starr taking photographs of one another during a break in the shooting of the film Magic Christian *in June 1969.*

195 Peter Sellers and Ringo Starr in a photo taken on February 22nd, 1969.

his MBE to protest against Great Britain's involvement in the Nigeria-Biafra conflict and the war in Vietnam. The pair's dedication to peace led John and Yoko to wage an international campaign in which they placed gigantic posters in twelve major cities of the world bearing the following statement: "War is over, if you want it."

196 John Lennon and Yoko Ono at a press interview concerning anti-Vietnam War protests. Yoko holds a flyer from their pacifist campaign, while John shows his Bag of Laughs, which made the sound of guffaws when shaken.

196-197 During their honeymoon, John and Yoko held a "Bed-In" as a demonstration for peace. It took place in their room at the Hilton Hotel in Amsterdam.

5

THE END OF THE GREAT ADVENTURE, AND THE WORLD WITHOUT THE FAB FOUR

The Beatles resumed work on *Get Back* in mid-December of 1969 to try to salvage the album. At this point, it was planned to be the soundtrack of the documentary *Let It Be* directed by Lindsey-Hogg. The first attempt to finish the record had been entrusted to sound engineer Glyn Johns, but this didn't work out, so John made two other attempts, the first in December and the second between December and January. He recorded by himself and added songs to the track list through early January 1970, including sessions on January 3rd and 4th at the Abbey Road studios. These two sessions were the last in which the Beatles played together. They recorded Harrison's "I Me Mine" and finished "Let It Be." But this attempt to finish the project was once again rejected by the band. Glyn Johns decided to try a second time, but the band remained unsatisfied.

MCCARTNEY DIDN'T CARE FOR PHIL SPECTOR'S WORK, ESPECIALLY CONCERNING TRACKS LIKE "LET IT BE" AND "THE LONG AND WINDING ROAD"

In March of 1970, John, George, and Ringo decided to ask the American producer Phil Spector to finish the work. This choice triggered a negative reaction on the part of McCartney, who didn't approve of Spector's work, especially concerning songs like "Let It Be" and "The Long and Winding Road." Despite his, the project was finally finished and given the title Let It Be. McCartney was left feeling isolated and depressed.

He began working at home with Linda on songs of his own and, when he felt he had accumulated enough tracks, he decided to record a solo album and release it on April 17th, 1970.

When the other three found out about the project, they tried to change McCartney's mind, because the Apple plan, organized a few weeks earlier, was to release Ringo's first solo album, *Sentimental Journey*, on March 27th and *Let It Be* shortly after that. Ringo went to Paul's house on March 31st and told him what the other three were thinking, and Paul reacted badly, going so far as to tell Ringo to leave his house. The date for the release of *McCartney* remained set at April 17th. On April 9th, in an announcement regarding the date of the album's release, Paul McCartney admitted he saw no reason why he should work with the band in the future. He believed there was no longer any possibility he would be able to write songs with Lennon, and he distanced himself from the new manager, Allen Klein. The following day, Don Short of *The Daily Mirror* put the following full-page headline in the newspaper: "Paul Quits the Beatles."

On April 14th, displeased with Spector's work, McCartney sent a letter to Allen Klein asking him to change the arrangements and not to make any further decisions without speaking to him first. But his letter arrived too late—twelve days after the final version of the album was sent to McCartney and the others (and too late to make any further changes).

202 Left to right: George, Ringo, Yoko, John, and Paul during a break in the production of the film Let It Be, *directed by Michael Lindsay-Hogg.*

203 The front page of the Daily Mirror on April 10th, 1970, with the news that Paul McCartney had decided to leave the band.

an intimate bioscopic experience with

THE BEATLES

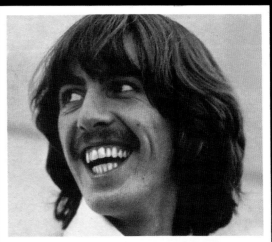

APPLE

An **abkco** managed company

presents

"Let it be"

As planned, on April 17th, Paul's first solo album was released, and May 8th saw the release of *Let It Be*, the Beatles' last record production. The documentary of the group recording the album won an Oscar, but the band no longer existed. By now, Paul had decided to sever all relations with everyone—John, George, Ringo, Klein, and Apple. He asked to leave the company. The others refused and, in the end, on December 30th, 1970, Paul filed a lawsuit against the other three demanding the dissolution of their partnership arrangement. Nothing definite occurred until 1973, partly because Lennon, Harrison, and Starr no longer had any interactions with Paul. The three no longer worked together either, and they soon stopped speaking to Klein. When the three finally lost trust in their manager, they fired him, and negotiations with Paul began in earnest. At last, in December of 1974, the four signed a

THE FORMAL DISBANDING OF THE BEATLES BECAME OFFICIAL ON JANUARY 9TH, 1975. It was the end of a legendary story

deal known as the Beatles Agreement. The formal disbanding of the Beatles became official on January 9th, 1975. Twenty years later, McCartney, Harrison, and Starr returned for the first time to work as the Beatles on releasing their monumental *The Beatles Anthology*. On that occasion, by utilizing John's incomplete recordings, they again recorded two pieces together, "Free as a Bird" and "Real Love"—the last episode of their story. And we're fortunate it's such a legendary story—the marvelous, musical adventure of a band that millions of us still love unconditionally.

204 The poster for the movie Let It Be. *The accompanying album features the same tracks as the movie. This was the last Beatles album released, though its material had been recorded before the songs for the album* Abbey Road.

THE AUTHOR

ERNESTO ASSANTE became a journalist in 1977. During a career spanning over 30 years, he has contributed articles to many Italian and foreign weeklies and monthlies including *Epoca, L'Espresso,* and *Rolling Stone.* He created and oversaw the supplements *Musica, Computer Valley,* and *Computer, Internet e Altro* for the Italian daily *La Repubblica.* Assante has also written books on music criticism, often in collaboration with his colleague Gino Castaldo. Since 2005, Assante and Castaldo have hosted *Lessons in Rock: Journey to the Center of Music,* a series of multimedia presentations with the aim of delving into the history of the legendary figures of rock music. From 2003 to 2009, Assante taught at Sapienza University in Rome. His classes included Theory and Technique of New Media and Analysis of Musical Languages. Among his numerous books on music, the following are published by White Star Publishers: *Legends of Rock, Masters of Rock Guitar, 5 Seconds of Summer, The Milestones of Rock & Roll: The Events That Changed the History of Music, U2: Past, Present, Future,* and *Woodstock: The 1969 Rock and Roll Revolution.*

Photo Credits

Page 5: Fiona Adams/Getty Images

Page 7: Mirrorpix

Pages 12-13: John Rodgers/Redferns/Getty Images

Page 19: Keystone/Getty Images

Page 24: GAB Archive/Redferns/Getty Images

Pages 24-25: K&K ULF KRUGER OHG/Redferns

Page 26: Ellen Piel – K & K/Redferns/Getty Images

Pages 26-27: Michael Ochs Archives/Getty Images

Page 34: Hulton Archive/Getty Images

Page 35: Michael Ochs Archives/Getty Images

Page 36: Keystone France/Gamma-Keystone/Getty Images

Pages 38-39: Harry Hammond/V&A Images/Getty Images

Page 41: Harry Hammond/V&A Images/Getty Images

Page 42: CBW/Alamy Stock Photo

Page 43: INTERFOTO/Alamy Stock Photo

Pages 44-45: © Hulton-Deutsch Collection/CORBIS/Corbis/Getty Images

Page 47: © Norman Parkinson/Iconic Images/Getty Images

Pages 48-49: Mirrorpix

Page 50: Michael Webb/Getty Images

Pages 50-51: Mirrorpix

Page 52: PixMix Images/Alamy Stock Photo

Page 53: Michael Ochs Archives/Getty Images

Page 54-55: Central Press/Getty Images

Page 55: David Farrell/Redferns/Getty Images

Pages 56-57: Mirrorpix

Pages 58-59: Mirrorpix

Page 60: Mirrorpix

Pages 60-61: Mirrorpix

Page 62: Mirrorpix

Pages 62-63: Mirrorpix

Page 64 top: Mirrorpix

Page 64 bottom: Mirrorpix

Page 65: Mirrorpix

Page 66: John Dominis/The LIFE Premium Collection/Getty Images

Page 67: Michael Ochs Archives/Getty Images

Page 68: Mirrorpix

Page 69: Mirrorpix

Page 70: Mirrorpix

Page 71: Mirrorpix

Page 72: Mirrorpix

Page 73: Mirrorpix

Pages 74-75: Unknown/Mirrorpix/Getty Images

Page 75: Mirrorpix

Pages 76-77: Mirrorpix

Page 77: Mirrorpix

Page 78: Mirrorpix

Pages 80-81: Bettmann/Getty Images

Page 82: Mirrorpix

Page 83: Mirrorpix

Page 84: Mirrorpix

Page 85: Mirrorpix

Page 86: Bob Gomel/The LIFE Images Collection/Getty Images

Pages 86-87: John Loengard/The LIFE Picture Collection/Getty Images

Page 88: Mike Smith/Pix Inc./The LIFE Images Collection/Getty Images

Page 89: Keystone/Getty Images

Page 91: Bettmann/Getty Images

Pages 92-93: Mirrorpix

Page 93: Mirrorpix

Pages 94-95: John Springer Collection/CORBIS/Corbis/Getty Images

Page 95: Max Scheler - K & K/Redferns/Getty Images

Pages 96-97: Mirrorpix

Page 98: Mirrorpix

Pages 98-99: Mirrorpix

Pages 100-101: Mirrorpix

Page 101: Mirrorpix

Pages 102-103: Mirrorpix

Page 104: Michael Ochs Archives/Getty Images

Page 105: Marc Tielemans/Alamy Stock Photo

Page 106: Michael Ochs Archives/Getty Images

Page 107: Mirrorpix

Page 108: David Pollack/Corbis/Getty Images

Page 111: Mirrorpix

Page 112: Mirrorpix

Page 113: Mirrorpix

Page 114: Robert Whitaker/Getty Images

Page 116: Philippe Le Tellier/Paris Match/Getty Images

Page 117 top: CBW/Alamy Stock Photo

Page 117 bottom: Michael Ochs Archives/Getty Images

Page 118: Blank Archives/Getty Images

Page 119: Michael Ochs Archives/Getty Images

Pages 120-121: Ted West/Central Press/Hulton Archive/Getty Images

Page 121: Central Press/Getty Images

Pages 122-123: William Vanderson/Fox Photos/Hulton Archive/Getty Images

Page 124: Buyenlarge/Getty Images

Page 125: Mirrorpix

Pages 126-127: Hulton Archive/Getty Images

Page 128: Mirrorpix

Pages 128-129: Mirrorpix

Page 130: PA Images/Getty Images

Page 131: Express Newspapers/Getty Images

Page 132: Imagno/Getty Images

Pages 132-133: Mirrorpix

Page 134: REPORTERS ASSOCIES/Gamma-Rapho/Getty Images

Pages 134-135: REPORTERS ASSOCIES/Gamma-Keystone/Getty Images

Page 140: Bettmann/Getty Images

Page 141: Bettmann/Getty Images

Page 142: MPVCVRART/Alamy Stock Photo

Page 143: Roger Viollet Collection/Getty Images

Pages 144-145: Keystone Features/Getty Images

Page 146: K & K Ulf Kruger OHG/Redferns/Getty Images

Pages 146-147: Otfried Schmidt/ullstein bild/getty Images

Page 148: Bob Whitaker/Hulton Archive/Getty Images

Page 149: Robert Whitaker/Getty Images

Page 150: Mark and Colleen Hayward/Redferns/Getty Images

Page 151: Bettmann/Getty Images

Page 154 top: Mirrorpix

Page 154 bottom: Mirrorpix

Page 156: dcphoto/Alamy Stock Photo

Page 158: John Downing/Getty Images

Page 159: Mirror Syndication International/Mirrorpix/Mirrorpix/Getty Images

Page 160: Bettmann/Getty Images

Page 161: Michael Ochs Archives/Getty Images

Page 162: Keystone Features/Hulton Archive/Getty Images

Pages 162-163: Mirrorpix

Page 164: David Redferns/Redferns/Getty Images

Page 165: Cummings Archives/Redferns/Getty Images

Page 166: PictureLux/The Hollywood Archive/Alamy Stock Photo

Page 167: TCD/Prod.DB/Alamy Stock Photo

Page 168: Evening Standard/Hulton Archive/Getty Images

Page 169: CBW/Alamy Stock Photo

Pages 170-171: HultonArchive/Getty Images

Page 172: Stroud/Express/Getty Images

Page 173: Andrew Maclear/Hulton Archive/Getty Images

Pages 174-175: Pictorial Press Ltd/Alamy Stock Photo

Page 175: Blank Archives/Getty Images

Page 176: Photo 12/Alamy Stock Photo

Page 177: Photo 12/Alamy Stock Photo

Page 178: John Reader/The LIFE Images Collection/Getty Images

Page 179: © Collection Gregoire/Bridgeman Images

Page 180: Blank Archives/Getty Images

Page 181: ODD ANDERSEN/AFP/Getty Imges

Page 182: Koh Hasebe/Shinko Music/Getty Images

Page 183: Andrew Maclear/Redferns/Getty Images

Page 184: SSPL/Getty Images

Page 185: John Pratt/Getty Images

Pages 186-187: Bettmann/Getty Images

Pages 188-189: Express/Express/Getty Images

Page 190: Bettmann/Getty Images

Page 191: Daily Herald/Mirrorpix/Mirrorpix/Getty Images

Page 192: Pictorial Press Ltd/Alamy Stock Photo

Page 194: Mirrorpix

Page 195: Keystone-France/Gamma-Keystone/Getty Images

Page 196: Bettmann/Getty Images

Pages 196-197: © Hulton-Deutsch Collection/CORBIS/Corbis/Getty Images

Page 202: Album/Contrasto

Page 203: Mirrorpix

Page 204: Movie Poster Image Art/Getty Images

Project editor

Valeria Manferto De Fabianis

Graphic design

Paola Piacco

EDIZIONI WHITE STAR

WS White Star Publishers® is a registered trademark property of White Star s.r.l.

© 2019 White Star s.r.l.
Piazzale Luigi Cadorna, 6 - 20123 Milan, Italy
www.whitestar.it

Translation: Richard Pierce - Editing: Leo Costigan

ISBN 978-88-544-1534-8
2 3 4 5 6   25 24 23 22 21

Printed in Italy